G000167154

Tempus ORAL HISTORY *Series*

Winchester
voices

The Itchen Navigation near Winchester, 1978. (HCLS).

Tempus ORAL HISTORY *Series*

Winchester
voices

Compiled by
Sarah Bussy

TEMPUS

First published 2002
Copyright © Sarah Bussy, 2002

Tempus Publishing Limited
The Mill, Brimscombe Port,
Stroud, Gloucestershire, GL5 2QG

ISBN 0 7524 2447 5

Typesetting and origination by
Tempus Publishing Limited
Printed in Great Britain by
Midway Colour Print, Wiltshire

Domum Cottage on the Itchen Navigation, 1978. Gertrude Asher was born here in 1880. (HCLS)

Contents

Introduction

This picture of life in Winchester between the 1880s and the 1950s would not have been possible if the late Austin Whitaker, then the City Archivist, had not begun to make a series of recordings of its elderly inhabitants as early as 1969. Further recordings were made by myself and others and have been added to the collection which is held in the Wessex Film and Sound Archive at the Hampshire Record Office.

One of those interviewed was Gertrude Asher. She was born in 1880 at Domum Cottage beside the Itchen Navigation (or 'the canal' as it was known locally) and through family recollections can take us back to when her grandfather worked on it bringing goods up from Northam[1]. Her grandmother recalled coming from West Meon to live in Winchester at a time when the trees on the Lawn had just been felled prior to the eventual construction of Eastgate Street. Her mother spoke of a time before the Didcot Newbury and Southampton Railway brought trains into Chesil Station[2] and before Highcliffe estate was begun. In 1886 Gertrude's family moved into one of the first houses to be built there. There was just a rough road, no church or school and they lived surrounded by cornfields. Arthur Warren was born one year after Gertrude and as a boy enjoyed playing in the meadows. He recalls the building of the viaduct[3] across them. 'It ruined the meadows' he said. 'We all thought that'.

Listening to the recordings you realise not only how close the countryside was, but how important the natural environment as a whole was to people. All children, regardless of social background, could share the same freedoms and pleasures within it. When they weren't at school or having to make themselves useful in some way they could splash around in the river or go off to the woods to collect nuts, mushrooms or primroses. Sometimes, as Joan Halford did, they made themselves useful and enjoyed themselves at the same time by taking a pram and collecting firewood. And for many families, Sunday afternoon was always spent walking on the surrounding downs or picnicking on St Catherine's Hill or elsewhere.

Although to some extent older patterns of life can be seen to continue until the 1950s or later, change of all kinds was inevitable throughout a period which felt the impact of two world wars and witnessed the arrival of the motor car. In fact in 1984, when Ernest Woolford was eighty he said he felt as if he had lived in three different times – before 1914, between the wars and after 1945. Before the advent of the motor car, Winchester seems to have been a particular world of its own and within that world there were other worlds, as you will hear described later. One of them was the College, and although between the wars it was perceived to be effectively cut off from the city, this had not always been so. There had been a time before 1914 when the cricket match against Eton was a source of interest, excitement or profit for virtually everyone in the town. When it was played at home, houses were let to visiting parents, the townspeople put on their best clothes to go along and watch while the tradesmen put great ingenuity into dressing their shop windows.

Comparing life in 1977 with how she knew it earlier in the century, Ann Dagleish said,

'You could sum it up really by saying that it wasn't necessary to be very wealthy or out of the top drawer. We enjoyed a little graciousness of living with very little money and not much of a position.' While this was undoubtedly true for many people and was probably one reason why Winchester was an attractive place for retirement, there was nothing gracious about conditions in some of the back streets. When people enjoyed what the High Street had to offer in terms of its commodities, services, deference and personal attention, it was apparently possible to ignore the squalor that lay just yards behind it.

In the selection I have made, we hear from some of those who lived in such places. We also hear from professional people and from the sons and daughters of former mayors. Among others, we hear from the craftsman, the builder, the coal man, the labourer, the housewife, the shop assistant and the gardener. They speak of their schooldays, work, family and social life and the importance of religion. They tell us about Winchester in wartime and about matters specific to the city. They tell us what it meant to be a Wintonian but at the same time often record a way of life common elsewhere in England at that time.

Some interviewees express regret about changes that have taken place while others do not. Personally I cannot help feeling sad when I imagine the beauty of Winchester's surrounding landscape a hundred or more years ago. I also feel a sense of loss in relation to the countless people whose lives have gone unrecorded and who could have given us a much fuller picture of how life in Winchester used to be. And although we see glimpses in the book of terrible hardship and personal tragedy, we have none of the darkest side of life represented for example by the workhouse and the prison. There is much that is missing but nevertheless I think there is sufficient material here for the reader to decide which changes are to be mourned and which are cause for celebration.

Sarah Bussy

A date in square brackets within an extract gives the year in which a recording was made.

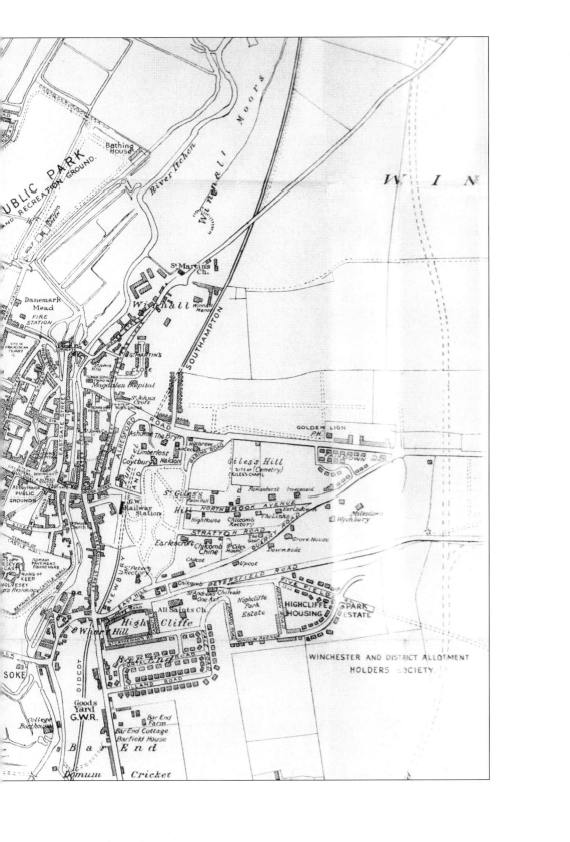

CHAPTER 1

Aspects of the City and its People

One large Community

Everybody seemed to be more sociable to one another and you were just one large community. We knew almost everyone we saw in the street. People had deeper roots in those days. In this terrace [on the Alresford Road] people lived for generations and brought up their families. It was the same in St John's Road.

May O'Neill, born c. 1900

At New Year as the cathedral bells rang, all the people in the Brooks[4] would come out of their doors and if the weather was fine they would go down outside the Guildhall. They would form a huge circle that went all round King Alfred's statue and up the Broadway. They would all join hands and sing *Auld Lang Syne*. There would be bands turn out and everyone would be singing and dancing in the Broadway at midnight.

Joan Halford, née Edmonds, 1926

Who was who

On the one hand there was the town life which was something in itself. The people had been here for generations. They'd been to school together, they knew each other, they'd done it all together – joined the army, played sport, married each others sisters and what not. It was a very close-knit thing. If you went down the High Street on a Saturday night the place was alive. Every pub was packed. People were rushing in and out from one to the other seeing their friends. There used to be two or three wild women who'd start at the top of the High Street and work their way down the pubs. You know, it was really something. You could enjoy yourself. You were in a place that was alive. All sorts of scandals… On the other hand, Winchester was divided into the City Council, the Chamber of Commerce, the College, the Cathedral and the Barracks. They were separate entities who might meet on the odd occasion.

Leslie Greenslade, born c. 1915

You got the Cathedral which was a law unto itself, and you got the College which was even more a law unto itself – practically a closed book in those days. It's only really since the Second World War that the College has come out more into the town and the town has gone more into the College. It was – I won't say monastic – but completely enclosed and secluded. The scholars weren't allowed to come into the town. Or very, very little. The staff and so forth were very much a community amongst themselves. Then there was the fraternity of the Hampshire Regiment and the two Rifle Regiments – the King's Royal Rifles and the Rifle Brigade.

Monica Woodhouse, née Stroud, 1911

The High Street

My chief recollection of Winchester early in the century is of the High Street. You came down from the Westgate quietly. There was no rush and no crowds. There was Salmon's, a lovely photographer's. Across the road was Hodder's, a furnishers with beautiful furniture. You wandered down the street and the people who owned the shops were characters who belonged to the city. It was alive. It was a city to which you belonged. I can see Dyer's, the grocer's, and the God Begot. Miss Pamplin owned the God Begot which was one of the most famous hotels in the world then. My memory of Winchester is the quietness of it,

Looking westward up the High Street towards the Westgate, c. 1911. (HRO 41M93/47/27)

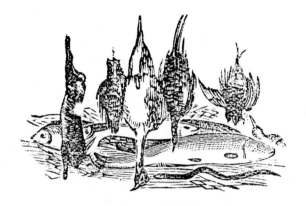

ZEBEDEE Z. BUTCHER,

Fishmonger, Poulterer, and Dealer in Game,

143, HIGH STREET, WINCHESTER.

Warren's Winchester Directory, 1906.

irrespective of the two wars. You could walk on the heads of the Americans in the Second World War but nevertheless it's only in latter years that it's become noisy and characterless.

Ann Dagleish

In the High Street before the first war, there were a number of those beautiful bow windows. There was one that was a very high-class grocery belonging to Alderman Dyer. He had a magnificent double bow window. And there used to be a fishmonger of very high repute. His name was Zebedee Zephania Butcher, and he was the most charming old man to look at. A real old patriarch and so very

attentive. I was taken for walks in the High Street with my governess or shopping with my mother. The individual shopkeepers, they kind of took notice of us as children you know. You went there as if perhaps you were going to a friend's.

Beatrice Forder

The shops were not large but they all contributed to the atmosphere. They were really rather upper class people or thought they were. Things were very reasonable; they were cheap in fact. Yet all the tradesmen were very comfortably off. They had big houses up on St Giles Hill. Take the Coopers at the Mercantile Stores. I remember when old man Cooper died, and my father saying with bated breath, 'I should think he's died worth ten thousand.' They were all worth ten thousand that lot.

Ann Dagleish

When we came here in 1934, most of the shops in the High Street were privately owned and all the owners were in a club in a kind of way. They all intermarried – the Sherriffs, the Browns, the Cliftons, the Butts, and the Hayters. It was all individual people. There was Ross the jeweller and Mr Savage who ran a very nice upholstery shop. You went to separate shops for separate things. We had about six drapers. If you wanted a reel of cotton or something and if you didn't find it at one shop you had the choice of the others. Now [1977] we've got Woolworth's or Debenham's. The atmosphere was quite different because they were pleased to serve you. They didn't throw things at you. The incredible thing was how long you kept your staff. We had a chef at the Stanmore Hotel for thirty years and we had Mabel for twenty-five. We had them all for over twenty-five years and it was exactly the same in the High Street. The buyer in Edmonds or Brown's, and the people that sold you your stockings – it was the same people always. Although they said they were badly paid, they stayed in their jobs and were happy working. They were content.

Muriel Taylor

I can remember gorgeous ices at Collis, Cobb and Spencer's. Real cream ices. I've never had one since except in Spain. And Clifton's were very superior tailors. I could just afford one suit a year. Their price was three guineas for a ladies tailor-made suit. But I didn't have to pay three guineas because I explained to Clifton's that I was so tiny they didn't need as much material. I always got my suits from Clifton's at two and a half guineas. I even had my wedding clothes and my going-away clothes made there. Comparing life now [1977] with life earlier in the century, you could sum it up really by saying that it wasn't necessary to be very wealthy, or out of the top drawer. We enjoyed a little graciousness of living with very little money and not much of a position

Ann Dagleish

Talking of Clifton's, I still have [1977] a pair of cavalry twill trousers I bought from there. They're so heavy and stiff that they very nearly stand up by themselves, and I think I bought those just before the war. It was when trousers inclined towards the Oxford Bag type. There's so much material in them it would make two pairs now.

Cyril Taylor

I remember when Woolworth's first opened in 1929. I went and bought my first bathing suit there. It was a navy blue one with white edging, and I got that for sixpence.

Irene Underwood, née Clewer, 1916

We remember so well the George Hotel. For children that was the grandest place. It had a palm court. There were parties there

The Palm Court at the George Hotel. (WMS)

and we used to think it was very grand. You drove right into it and then out into St George's Street.

Amy Stidston, Ruth Stackard (sisters),
née Savage

When we first came to Winchester in 1934, we took ourselves out for the evening and we went to the old George Hotel. The entrance was really Dickensian where the carriages used to go in. It had an in and an out – a front and a back entrance. Individual businessmen used to meet there at lunchtime, but they never used to like people to know that they went in so they slid in at the back. I could name them now... And Dumper's was a lovely place to go for a morning coffee. One dressed up to go to coffee. Put on a fur and a hat. You didn't go down town without dressing up.

Muriel Taylor

At the Mercantile Stores you could buy anything from a packet of pins to a fur coat. In fact if your change was a farthing, they gave you a packet of pins instead. The money you paid was wrapped in a bill and put in a sort of wooden cup which had two parts twisted together, and sent along a wire to a central till manned by a couple of girls. They put the bill on a spike and sent the cup back to the counter with your change in it. At the Maypole shop they had great mounds of butter, and a man with butter pats chopped off a bit, patted it about and plonked it on the scales. My mother used to ask for a taste, which was duly offered to her on the end of a big knife. I remember that they thought the manager there was a German, and when the war broke out in 1914 he had to hide in the cellar because people were after his blood. Foster's the tobacconist had bare boards on the floor, quite small brass scales for weighing tobacco and a gas jet from which customers could light their cigarettes and pipes.

Dorothy Yaldren, née Newman, 1903

Edmonds – just opposite the Buttercross – they knocked out those bow windows that had been in Dyer's and before that in Hales and Blake and made an extension to their shop. Winchester people were disgusted by a display of ladies stockings – a sort of rotating set of legs that were hardly decent. If you wanted to get haberdashery you went to Sherriff and Ward's, and slightly higher up the scale to Brown's. In Brown's, wherever you went you had shopwalkers. Very elegant men they were wearing striped trousers and morning coats, and if you weren't

receiving proper attention the head floorwalker would say, 'Forward Mr Smith' or 'Forward Miss Jones.'

William H.C. Blake, born 1905

Next to St Maurice's church there was a family butcher named Wright. Any big thing that was on like the Coronation of George V, he roasted a bullock. He had a big fire on top of St Giles Hill and he gave a roasted bullock. Dumper's, who had a shop at the corner of Market Street, they gave the rolls. They cut the bullock up in slices and everyone had a slice of bullock between a roll cut in half. Bit smoky but it went down very good.

Richard Pearce, born 1893

Before World War One we had these German bands of about forty to fifty. They used to send round the hat, and the music was quite pleasing. The only other bands we had round here were the military ones which were always going up and down the street. The Germans were all rounded up during the war and never came back afterwards. There were a great number of barrel organs too at one time. There were three brothers who operated one for over forty years. Then there were the Italian organ grinders, who always had little monkeys with red jackets on. I suppose these Italians used to live in cheap lodging houses.

William H.C. Blake, born 1905

Go down town at quarter to twelve on a Saturday night, you could get half a cow for about a shilling because they had no cold storage for it. That's when the shopping was done. The High Street was one blaze of lights on a Saturday night and there was more shopping done between ten o' clock and midnight than any other time probably.

Reginald O'Neill, born c. 1903

About Christmas time, Page and Phillips used to have all the turkeys hanging right from the roof to the ground outside on metal racks. All these magnificent turkeys. Poor Seymour the Health Inspector would have kittens if they did this now [1977].

Muriel Taylor

Butchers or poultry shops would be working more or less from four o'clock in the morning until eleven o'clock at night. It was nothing to see the butchers cutting up their meat at four o' clock in the morning getting ready to open at six or seven o'clock.

Cyril Taylor

Where the Meat and Poultry came from

Every Monday the farmers used to walk to Winchester, driving their animals to the livestock and poultry market, which was held behind the old Corn Exchange where the public library is now. The

Mr Wright the butcher in the doorway of his shop at 16 High Street. (HRO41M93/47/7)

butchers bought the animals they wanted and then they took them along Jewry Street towards the High Street, down St George's Street which was just a little lane then, and on to the different slaughterhouses. Living in the Brooks, it was great fun for us children because as soon as we came out of school on Monday teatime it would be time for them to be herded down there. When they got to Parchment Street, Upper Brook Street, Middle Brook Street and Lower Brook Street the animals would try to go off into these areas. They would try to do a bunk. They often used to run up the Brooks and of course us kids used to run like mad and scream and shout and carry on something terrible if a cow got loose and came charging after us. I think the animals had a sense that they were going to be killed, because they would all try to bolt. As they got near the slaughterhouse they could smell the death and the blood.

Joan Halford, née Edmonds, 1926

Drink and Disorder

There were five pubs in Wharf Hill alone. You could throw a stone and hit every one; The Miller's Arms, The Black Boy, The Duke's Head, The Dog and Duck and The King's Arms.

Herbert North, born 1906

The Suffolk Arms⁵ used to be the rendezvous for the gypsies. Every Saturday they used to congregate there. They would park their horses and carts at the back, and finish up every Saturday

night with a fight. The police had a good time clearing them off.

Richard Pearce, born 1893

Before the first war when I was about seven, I remember going to St John's Rooms with my parents. I had been allowed to see Lady Little who was a midget. When we came up the High Street afterwards Dad kept telling me not to look, so of course I looked and it was a soldier being frog-marched from one of the pubs. It always stuck in my mind. It was horrible.

Phyllis Richardson, née Spire, 1905

That sort of thing was a nightly occurrence. It was a favourite way of taking troops who misbehaved themselves. One soldier or policeman on each arm and one on each leg. He was face downwards and couldn't get away.

Stanley Richardson, born 1906

There really were some pretty frightful pubs in Winchester early in the century. They were beer houses just for drinking.

William H.C. Blake, born 1905

There was much drunkenness, with the resulting quarrelling and fighting. It was a common sight to see a man staggering from one side of the road to the other. Sometimes they fell down and continued crawling for a while, until some kind person helped them rise and assisted them home.

William Blackman, born 1908

Looking eastward down the High Street early in the twentieth century. Part of the George Hotel is just visible on the left. (HCLS)

Roads, Streets, Transport and Traffic

It was all horses and carts, and they done more work with them than what they do with motors. Coal was taken round in carts and if you didn't think it was what you thought was standard, we come and took it all back. I worked from seven in the morning to seven at night, Monday to Friday, and from seven in the morning until nine at night on Saturday. You had carriers coming here from Stockbridge, Cheriton, Alresford, Chandlers Ford, Owslebury and any amount of places.

Arthur W. Hodges, born 1888

The carriers used to come in from all the country districts up to a radius of about eight miles. They used to mostly pull into what was the Coach and Horses (which was where Sainsbury's is now), or at the India Arms. They'd arrive in the city about eleven o' clock in the morning. They'd stay there while people did their shopping. People would go to and fro, bringing their parcels back to put them in the cart and then between four and six o' clock, depending on the distance they had to travel, you'd see them all leaving Winchester going in different directions. Most villages had at least one carrier.

Reginald O'Neill, born c. 1903

The Black Swan Hotel used to run a very good horse and bus service. They used to run around the town. You just had to tell them you wanted to go to the station, and they used to come round and collect you up with this horse and bus and charge you sixpence. That was the only public transport in the town. The horse buses came on later. A man named Blake started to run them. He ran them from Twyford turning to the Corn Exchange – tuppence a ride. It was a great help to St Cross people because you had to walk everywhere you see. The country people had to walk in too from Compton, Shawford and everywhere. The only road transport between Winchester and Southampton was the carrier, and he used to start at the Coach and Horses at the bottom of the town. He would start there in the morning and go down to Southampton every day. He'd carry any parcel for threepence or sixpence a time according to the size of it, and passengers if you wanted to go. But he only went at a jog trot pace. At one time you could go to Southampton by train for a shilling return.

Richard Pearce, born 1893

Michaelmas was the time when all the farmhands used to change if they wanted another job. They used to go up to the market in Jewry Street, and stand outside the Corn Exchange on market day. They put themselves up for hire. To show what he was offering, each man used to wear an emblem in his coat. A carter used to wear a whipcord and a thatcher used to have a little bundle of straw in his coat. They all had different ways of showing what their different trades was. If a farmer was wanting someone he used to go up to these men, and if they were suitable he used to engage them. Then he would send his horse and wagon to collect their furniture and move them over. It was all done at Michaelmas time. All you could see along the road was farm wagons full of furniture. Something of everything in them. Chickens, dogs, cats – everything was on the wagon.

Richard Pearce, born 1893

If you look at some of the early photographs of Winchester High Street you will see how rough the surface was. They had crossing sweepers clearing a way from one pavement to another, and the people who were crossing gave them a little something for their labours. In the early days of the Scouts, that would be 1907 or 1908, we would march along the Petersfield Road – as much as eight miles in an evening – and wouldn't see a vehicle, and just hear the crunch of our feet on the gravel and the twittering of a bird or two in the hedge. Lovely and peaceful. No motor horns and all the horses bedded down for the night. It might be interesting to know that the hedges weren't all green in summer but white with dust. The tarring of the roads and the abolition of dust seems to have gone unnoticed. The roads were just gravel rolled with the steamroller and watered in. When you did come across a motor car, you could see it miles away in clouds of dust. I often stood in Highcliffe and saw the cars coming over Cheesefoot Head like that.

Austin Laverty, born 1896

Telephone 0492.

R. MARTIN & SON,

Fly Proprietors and Job Masters,

CARRIAGES, BRAKES, G.W. OMNIBUS,
BATH CHAIR, GOVERNESS CART, ETC.

96, CHEESEHILL STREET,
AND
67, KINGSGATE STREET,

} WINCHESTER.

CHARGES MODERATE.

Warren's Winchester Directory, 1906.

As the streets weren't tarmacked in those days they were very dusty and it was lovely when the water cart went along. To a child it was always summer and always hot. One can smell the scent now when those water carts went along laying the dust. We remember the quietness of the streets in Winchester as well as the carriages drawing up outside the tradesmen's shops in the High Street. The fishmonger or whoever it was would go out to the carriage. The lady wouldn't trouble to get out at all. A certain class of people did their shopping like that. The carriages were mostly quite little – dog carts, you know – but you sometimes saw a victoria or a landau. Of course you could use a cab. There was a cab rank outside the County Club in Southgate Street and another outside the Roman Catholic church. I expect there was one in the Broadway too.

Amy Stidston, Ruth Stackard (sisters),
née Savage

In Bridge Street there was the Bridge Inn. It was a very fine inn, run by a man called Tom Wallace. His daughter Ada used to help him – a very popular, buxom lass. Behind the inn was a large yard which was shared by Mr Martin the fly proprietor. I was always intrigued with his horses and the men that had charge of them. At five o'clock they were all in their stables being watered and fed and being bedded down for the night. That was when the men got to work and washed their carriages. They used to get the water from the river with a bucket on a rope and haul it up to get on with the job. They didn't use water from the mains.

Austin Laverty, born 1896

They used to take the coal from the railway goods yard down North Walls several times a day in a horse-drawn lorry. Only one horse incidentally, but it was down hill. They could afford to use only one horse because they skidded it down Station Hill. Then they took the skids out going along City Road and put them on again down North Walls. The poor horse would be leaning backwards to keep the lorry from actually pushing it down the hill. It used to clump and clatter down there. Sparks used to come out of their hooves as the horses pressed backwards to hold back the great loads of coal.

Stanley Richardson, born 1906

Something that filled everyone with awe was the sight of the bus which took people to the hospital. Horse-drawn of course. The windows were all curtained and very mysterious. It struck fear in you as to what would happen to the person inside.

Beatrice Forder

The only ambulance I remember was just like a bier. Four-wheeled and propelled by a man in front and a man behind. It had a semi-circular waterproof sheet over the top.

Winchester Fire Brigade in 1907. (HRO 91M85W/1)

Stanley and Phyllis Richardson in 1961 at their son Barry's wedding. (EAS)

My father and mother, being Londoners, regarded Winchester as a country village, particularly as there were still oil lamps visible in the back streets. Most of the smaller streets were lit by gas and a man on a bicycle used to go round and light them. This he did very expertly by pushing a pole through an aperture at the base of the lantern, which simultaneously switched on the gas and lit it by means of flame inside a brass tube at the end of the pole. He rarely stopped his cycle but with the expertize of a pig-sticking lancer, he managed to carry out this amazing feat with nothing more than a clatter and a pop. At my age he seemed to be performing something of a miracle and I longed for the day when I would be old enough to become a lamp lighter.

Stanley Richardson, born 1906

If there'd been an accident, the person was popped in there and wheeled away and pushed up to the hospital.

Austin Laverty, born 1896

The fire station was at the side of the Guildhall. The engine was pulled by horses and they had to come right from the top station where they were stabled. They had to clump all down North Walls, around Eastgate Street to get to the engine. It was a long time before they were ready to get out to a fire. Then when the engine went out, a Mr Lassiter was the first man to light the fire. He always had bundles of chopped wood ready. They had to light a fire to get steam up to get the pump to work.

Alfred O'Neill, born c. 1896

Some of the gas lights were fuelled by sewer gas and so ventilated the sewers. They burnt day and night. There was one at the top of Sleepers Hill and there was one in the Square. You saw these lights on all day purposely, and during the Second World War they had to black them out.

Cyril Taylor

Memorable People

When we were living in the Brooks, every Saturday evening old Mrs Norris would bring dairy produce in. She used to come by pony and trap and come in with a very big white wicker basket on her arm and bring the butter and the eggs and things. I can see her now with a pointed shawl down her back and a big skirt and bobbing a curtsy as she went out of the door. I think she came from the Petersfield direction.

Beatrice Forder

The last buildings in Bridge Street in the foothills of St Giles Hill were owned by a man who was a clay pipe manufacturer. A man named Goodall. He used to make the clay pipes during the week, and on the Friday he would set forth with his four-wheeler drawn by a pony and deliver his goods. Throughout the city to start with. That would be to the barbers' shops and the tobacconists, and in those days you could see his churchwarden pipes in the tobacconists' windows and when he finished his city round he would make off then to the villages. He would be away a couple of nights and then he would return and go all through the motion again. He was a gentlemanly old fellow. A very jovial person.

Austin Laverty, born 1896

I started in the Scotch Wool Shop in 1917 and I left them forty-three years after. I was made manageress soon after I was twenty. I can remember one special little old lady, a widow who came in from the country every Wednesday and Friday. She came with these little pieces of paper, different orders which she had taken from the people out in the villages. I suppose it helped her to get a living and we used to give her what we could. She was a dear old soul. She did that for years and years.

May O'Neill, born c. 1900

Mr Stopher[6] lived on St Giles Hill. He was an outstanding character really, and when he was much over eighty he would come down to his office which was over the *Chronicle*. He only went to business in the morning when we remembered him. When he'd had his nap after lunch he would spend the afternoon in his library which was a sanctum. No one was allowed in there except by special invitation. He used to sit there working on his scrapbooks. He compiled many, many scrapbooks of local events. He was most fastidious about this. He loved St Giles Hill where, naturally, he saw the most wonderful skyscapes and sunsets. It was his habit to go out onto the hill and say 'Praise the Lord oh my soul! All that is within me praise His Holy Name!'. He would only walk up St Giles Hill by the steps. He thought it would be a great come-

Looking eastward down St George's Street from the junction with St Peter's Street, before 1956. (HCLS)

down to go round by the slope. But for the last year or two of his life he had to give in and go by the slope. I think it cost him quite a lot. He was rather an emotional man when he let himself go – very quickly moved to tears, and he used to say that he was born when cucumbers were in season!

Beatrice and Mildred Forder

Mr Henry and Mr Herbert Johnson were very well-known characters. You never went into the *Chronicle* office when Mr Herbert Johnson didn't appear. To all the customers he gave full attention. He was always there, or came forward and always accompanied you to the door and showed you out. Our father used to say that his motto was, 'Bow low and charge high'. He was perfect at his job really.

Beatrice and Mildred Forder

'Old Dad'[7] was a famous old chap. Well known all over the place, and I used to know him very well. He was an enormous old fellow and his trousers all bulged with parcels which were tied to his leg. Very few people knew that his name was Richardson; he was just known as 'Old Dad'. In the summer you could see him in the meadows below the city, done up like a Christmas tree, sitting there minus his boots and socks, dangling his feet in the pure crystal stream. He came to our Scout camp at Kings Worthy once. We put up our tent in a beautiful little paddock there. He said did we mind him staying there and we said, 'No, delighted!' He was installed in a very short time under a hawthorn bush just behind our tent. Two or three days later I offered him

some breakfast. We had cooked some rashers. I gave him a couple and he said, 'Thank you very much but they're not done you know. When you've finished with your fire I'll show you how to cook them'. He got these rashers on to a sheet of newspaper, one on top of the other, and folded the paper over and over and tucked in the ends. Then he scraped away the embers of our fire, put the paper on the hot base and covered it with the embers again. A little smoke came up and I thought well, there go a couple of really good rashers. I was proved wrong because in about a quarter of an hour's time he said, 'Well they're done now.' So I watched him carefully with apprehension. He scraped the embers away again, took out this black package, put it on a plate and carefully unwrapped it to reveal two lovely rashers – brown and oily and smelling perfect. I had to get back to school then but we left him with a twinkle in his eye, getting down to his breakfast. I'd never smelled such rashers in my life, never before or since.

Austin Laverty, born 1896

The most colourful character we knew was an old tramp who regularly came into Winchester. If you asked him where he lived he said, 'Number One Crab Wood.'

Jessie Canfield, née Dixon, 1903

There used to be some queer characters about the town. There was one old boy by the name of Cook; Cooky they used to call him. He had a wispy sort of moustache and beard and a very unfortunate nose – all sort of carbuncles. I think he used to disappear into the workhouse in the winter. Then in the summer he would appear with a clarinet and stand on the corner playing doleful tunes. There was another funny old woman they used to call Liz Bacon. Boys would call after her, 'Who stole the bacon?' and Liz would turn round and swear without repeating herself for about ten minutes. Those sort of people seem to have vanished. You don't see them about these days.

R.A. Judd, born 1894

Peters was the only negro one had ever seen in those days. I think he worked for the corporation. He used to drive a cart of some sort. It was a rare thing to have seen a negro. He was a very big man. A very nice man.

Amy Stidston, Ruth Stackard (sisters),
née Savage

The Reverend Dickens[8] was Rector of St John's. Interesting old chap. He used to ride in a sort of bath chair business with a pony. It ran away once down St John's Street with the old vicar and just when it got next to the grocer's shop it overturned and the vicar somehow got thrown out and was lying underneath the pony. However he wasn't too badly hurt, but that made him give up that sort of transport and then he went in for a wagonette with a coachman and footman.

Austin Laverty, born 1896

The Reverend Dickens had a vine out of doors and the grapes used to ripen. He'd invite us choirboys down and get us to put our caps out and he'd put a bunch in our

cap. Another time he'd get a big tub of ice cream down and dish it out to us. He was a nice old boy in a way, but I was nervous of him. If there was anything wrong he'd bellow. Shout at you. He soon lost his temper. There was a man used to live at Winnall had a traction engine, and he used to come up past the church with it. If there was a service on and that engine turned into the bottom of the street the Reverend Dickens would shut up the bible; 'Here endeth the lesson. Come off out!' Whether he was afraid the place was going to fall down I don't know but he wouldn't stay in the church. We all used to scoot off out. Most irreverent you might say. We just about ran and although he walked with a couple of sticks he almost kept up with us.

Jesse Smith, born 1903

William Walker[9] the Diver was a grand chap. Very solid looking. A very notable man. Everybody liked him. For children the great thing was to see the Diver come up because he'd been down in the bowels of the earth in mud and slime. These kids would goggle at him and he'd take his helmet off and say, 'Here I am. I'm all right'. He was a real jolly chap. It's owing to him that the cathedral stands up. The Queen and King George made quite a fuss of him, but I understand that the statue of him isn't him at all. [Mrs Elkins interjects, 'They got round that by saying it was symbolic!'] They had quite a celebration when that was unveiled in 1964. The Dean had thirty or forty members of the family turn up for the service and tea at the Deanery. One of the relatives was heard to say 'Well it's a nice statue but it ain't like our Dad.' Walker had a lovely black moustache and the statue

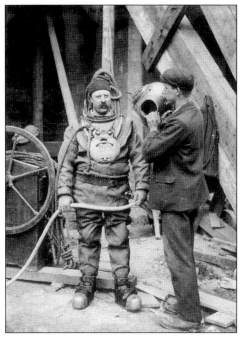

William Walker, the Diver. (WCL)

hasn't a moustache at all. The man who made the statue copied the wrong picture.

Reginald Elkins, born 1886

Poor old Aggie! She was one of the ladies of the town. She wasn't all that bad but she'd had a bit of bad luck. After she'd married a bloke it turned out he was full of TB and she wouldn't live with him. Then she lived on her own and she had to get a living some way. She used to work up the hospital as a cleaner and bring home fish heads that she found in the dustbins there. Then somebody must have said she was doing it, and the police caught her and put her in front of the magistrates here. She pleaded that all she wanted them for was for her cat. She didn't want them for her own self and they'd only have been chucked in the swill bin. But they wouldn't have that. She got a month inside. Just for that!

Victor Gough, born 1908

Sporty Ward always wore a square-topped bowler and he sat in this very high gig. He had a very smart little cob in front who knew the way home because when they were going home, Sporty was either asleep or singing. He was permanently drunk. When it was quiet you could hear the clip-clop of his cob coming along on the cobbles of Parchment Street from a long, long way. The worrying thing was when Sporty was drunk on the ice at Winnall. He was a good skater but he'd get into these thin patches and get very excited and nobody could get him out.

Stanley and Phyllis Richardson

Statue of the 'wrong man', Sir Francis Fox. (WCL)

Mrs Sparks the midwife was lovely she really was. She used to come in the morning and bath the baby and come in again in the evening to see to the mother and have a chat. She would bring you virtually your first dinner when you were allowed to eat properly. A chop or something. Otherwise you were on slops – bread and milk and gruel and all that for goodness knows how long. I was sorry when she went after my son was born. She was such a motherly old soul. Most particular but not too clinical. She was a marvellous woman, and very famous in Winchester for being a midwife. She lived there a long time in Colebrook Street and had about six or eight children of her own.

Lilian Woolford, née Hibberd, 1907

Miss Pamplin who used to keep the God Begot was quite a figure. She was rather autocratic and wore a long, sweeping dress and her hair piled up with a large hat on top. She wasn't at all a working restaurateur. She was very much the lady. On New Year's Day, the banks used to be closed while they cleared up their books for the year. Lloyds was opposite the God Begot and she always had them all over to a great feast in the evening. She had a good reputation for food and the God Begot was a very important feature in the town. There weren't so many places in which to eat in Winchester in those days.

Monica Woodhouse, née Stroud, 1911

Reading, Writing and Smoking Lounge at the God Begot, c. 1910 (WMS)

My uncle Austin Laverty was a keen voluntary guide for Winchester cathedral. In fact they used to hold a session where he would lecture on the woodwork of the cathedral for the benefit of the other guides. I suppose the craftwork of the Laverty family was at its height in the 1920s and 1930s. Wherever you looked you seemed to find examples of it. There was the large oak screen in the cathedral which was the work of quite a number of my uncles. I had eight, one of whom was killed in the Great War, and each of the uncles started his life in the business of Laverty's who were turners, carvers and makers of ecclesiastical furniture in particular. The large oak screen as I say was their work, and it was the combined work really of all the brothers of the family in some way or another. The large beam which carries the clock across Winchester High Street was the work of Edwin Laverty and so was the black swan which is now on the corner of Southgate Street. This was the black swan which was over the Black Swan Hotel, formerly on the site. The black swan incidentally is not painted wood. It is carved in ebony if you please, the kind of wood from which usually only small artefacts are made. To make a swan of this size must have taken quite a lot of time and quite a lot of sharpening of chisels.

Austin Underwood

Miss Firmstone was one of the first lady councillors. Father went to school with her at her father's school in Hyde Street. He always said she was the only girl about the place and the greatest tomboy. She became very masculine in her attire as she became older and her hair was rather short and brushed upwards. She did her best work among girls who wanted help. In the summer, she would stroll down Bull Drove with her bathing towel across her shoulder and the first thing she would do would be to go and get the thermometer and take the temperature. She wouldn't go in if it was under sixty. She used to tell a wonderful story against herself. During the first war when there were fewer street lights and she was walking home carrying a bag, a soldier followed her. He asked if he could carry her bag, which she allowed him to do but when they got underneath a street lamp he took one look at her, said, 'Good Lord!' dropped the bag and fled. She was very fond of this story.

Beatrice Forder

Then there was the time when the council put notices on the lamp posts saying 'Dogs must not foul the pavements' and Miss Firmstone remarked, 'Much too high! Dogs won't be able to read them.'

Monica Woodhouse, née Stroud, 1911

Archie Clements always took the buffoon's part in the Gilbert and Sullivan operas. He used to write a weekly half-column for us [in the *Hampshire Chronicle*] called 'Winchester Notes' and was a very good draughtsman. He used to draw cartoons. You'd find them on the old Gilbert and Sullivan programmes between the wars. The operatic things were a very great highlight in the life of Winchester, because there was nothing like the music that there is now.

Everybody went to that and there was an afternoon set aside for the County High School, the College and so on to go. I remember meeting someone who was formerly at the College and he said, 'Oh yes, you used to have to go to those so-and-so operettas didn't you? I used to have to suffer too!'

Monica Woodhouse, née Stroud, 1911

For a few years after the last war, until she died, I was employed as a gardener by Annette, Countess of Liverpool, who had bought a house in Courtenay Road. Her husband had been Governor General of New Zealand. She was one of the loveliest people I have ever met. She would ask me to take a seat and always addressed me as 'Mr Blackman' which was most unusual because the gentry seemed to have a thing about keeping you down. You were 'Blackman', or if you were young you were 'Will'am'. It was to keep you servile. But she wasn't like this one little bit. She would talk to all the road sweepers and the dustmen and share bullseyes with charladies on the bus.

William Blackman, born 1908

CHAPTER 2

Historical Events and Special Occasions

Running up the Bunting

There was a great deal of local patriotism I suppose you would might call it in those days. At any national celebration or local celebration, people would turn out in hundreds. They were very fond of processions and bunting was very quickly run up. There was such a keen interest taken by the inhabitants in what was taking place. I can remember the High Street with a display of flags for a royal birthday or any royal occasion or local occasion. People then took more interest in local affairs and if anything went on at the Guildhall, for instance if there was any regimental ceremony down there, the Broadway would be blocked with people. I took great interest in anything that was going on in front of the Guildhall.

Beatrice Forder

Queen Victoria's Golden Jubilee in 1887

When the Jubilee came we had a big tea party at school for all the children, and all the citizens of Winchester had a dinner in the Broadway. Tables were laid all down the Broadway and everybody went to this big dinner. A very grand dinner and it was served by Dumper's the big restaurant people. My mother went and she said they had lovely roast beef, roast pork, veal and ham and puddings and I don't know what. All laid out lovely down the Broadway there. All hot.

Gertrude Asher, née Whittier, 1880

A flying Visit from Queen Victoria in 1897

I never discovered why, but Queen Victoria disliked Winchester. However, when I was about ten, I remember her arriving at the station[10]. For some reason all the clergy were there in their robes, my father among them, and of course all the aldermen. One of the aldermen was a man called Shenton. He had a boy called Percy who was about my age. When the train drew in he hauled his little boy up on his shoulder, and at the same time Father motioned to a big policeman who then hauled me up onto his shoulder. When the old Queen arrived in the station the first thing she saw was these two children right above everybody else. She gave us a special smile I think. She was a funny little old person to look at. I was prepared for that but my brother who was a year younger was bitterly disappointed because she wasn't in a nightgown with a crown on.

Anne Madge, born 1887

The Boer War 1899-1902

After the relief of Mafeking, everybody was happy and went about waving flags. The College boys went over Longwood and came in on horseback waving flags.

Arthur W. Hodges, born 1888

I joined the Winchester Hockey Club with my brothers and Mafeking day we went over in a brake to play against Andover. On the way back we heard that Mafeking had been relieved and when we arrived in Winchester the whole place seemed to have gone mad altogether. We joined the crowd and the band played *Three Cheers for the Red, White and Blue* I think for about two hours without stopping. I've never experienced anything like it. We went about arm in arm through every street in Winchester playing *Three Cheers for the Red, White and Blue*. We seemed to be quite mental. I can hear the tune now.

Arthur Warren, born 1881

I well remember the men coming back from the Boer War. They stopped at Chesil Station and naturally they wanted to drink. They used to send the little boys with money to the pubs to get the beer for them, and a few of the lads of course they made a

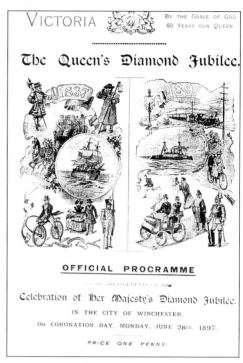

Diamond Jubilee Programme. (HRO 154M84W/5k)

penny or two for themselves. I remember an occasion when the boys had been sent off and the train had passed on before the boys got back with the goods. I don't know what happened to the beer.

Austin Laverty, born 1896

The Statue of King Alfred

I remember when King Alfred[11] was put up in 1901. My brother Don sang in the choir at the unveiling ceremony and I wish I had too. I remember seeing Alfred lying down in the goods yard at Chesil Station, outside the cattle pens. I guess he was there because it was the only place in the station where there was a crane. As for the plinth on which he

Procession of over 2,000 people from the Barrack Parade to the Cathedral on 28 June 1897.

(HRO 154M84W/5m)

stands, that had to come from the other station and they had to bring it from there on a low trolley, with wooden wheels about twenty four inches in diameter and about twenty inches thick. It was a slow business. When they did raise the bronze statue on top of the stone it was bedded down on sugar. The idea was so it would get a delicate sort of impact on contact with the stone. So they put the sugar there, watered it and it melted to gradually settle down in a compact mass below. Alfie was put on top of that. Remember they had no cranes. Just an ordinary tripod with a pulley-block, that's all. They had scaffold poles and if they weren't long enough or stout enough, they would rope them together to make them so.

Austin Laverty, born 1896

At the dedication of the statue I remember Lord Rosebery standing there with his frock coat and top hat – then pulling the curtains aside and unveiling it. An impressive ceremony.

Arthur Warren, born 1881

The Pageant of 1908

Winchester has never put on a show again like they did that pageant[12]. It was a wonderful thing. I went, we all went – everybody went. Historical it was and the way it was put on, the way it was acted and the singing and everything in it – it was a beautiful affair. People came from all over England to see that pageant. Funny thing, it was fine every day.

Richard Pearce, born 1893
Father was Mayor then of course. I should think that's one of my earliest recollections – that Mother was *always* out.

Mildred Forder, born 1904

The pageant was the very highlight of our lives. It brought everybody together. It was wonderful weather, and people just walked about the town in their costumes. All our family took part. There were four of us children and our parents were on the musical side of it. Actually we were quite disgusted because we were just Saxon townsfolk. I always remember Mr Stopher playing Sir Walter Raleigh. He was meant to be beheaded and the executioner was ready with his axe. It had been arranged that someone should gallop in at the last minute with a reprieve to stop the execution, but apparently they couldn't get the horse to start and so everybody, including Sir Walter and the executioner, had to sit around waiting. I saw all this and it was probably my earliest recollection.

Ruth Stackard, née Savage

Joe Dumper, the Gun Riots and the Pageant

The Gun Riots[13] might have appeared to most people to be a trivial affair, but the citizens of Winchester treated it all most seriously. The site where the gun was situated was treated as a speaker's corner where outdoor meetings could take place and it was frequently used at that time for temperance meetings and it was a favourite place for the Salvation Army to hold its services. Well the mayor and corporation were going to tidy up the city for the

Winchester National Pageant, and it had been mentioned on the council that the railings would be removed. The railings stood about four feet six inches high on a plinth of about eight inches, and they were put there really to prevent children climbing and perhaps meeting with an accident. Well, there was a protest immediately and a letter was sent to the mayor on the subject. It appeared that this letter did not get to the proper quarters and early one morning, the local Board men removed the railings. The railings were gone and most people were furious. So a protest meeting was organized that night at 7.30 p.m. and it was well advertised. I remember seeing the posters myself and they had a pony cart covered in posters that went round the town saying that there would be a protest meeting that night.

Well, promptly at 7.30 p.m., Mr Joe Dumper – who had organised the protest – arrived. He soon explained the situation and read out the names of the councillors responsible for the removal of the railings, making it clear to his listeners that these gentlemen should be ousted at the next council meeting. Hecklers said, 'What about the mayor?' Joe said, 'We will go round and see him presently.' His address was punctuated by blasts from a bugle and when a more popular phrase was quoted, the blasts were on an even grander scale. After his address, Joe said, 'I propose we now make a demonstration through the city.' So the crowd immediately lifted Joe shoulder-high and marched him to the mayor's house via Cross Keys Passage. However they were out-manoeuvred. They were forestalled because a dozen policeman were then lined up in front of the mayor's house together with the head constable. The mayor wasn't available.

Well, they broke a few windows there and

then went back to the Broadway to the gun, and the idea was to haul this gun through the streets. They got a rope on it and plenty of men. There was a builder's yard just adjacent, so there was no lack of ropes. Pulling it off the plinth, the barrel of the gun fell off. Well that just made room for Joe who used it as a chariot. He sat on the top and they hauled him along up the High Street and then the stones started to fly. Bricks through the town clock and bricks through every lamp. Every lamp was shattered. They went as far as the Black Swan building on the corner of Southgate Street and then turned down the street. There was a very loyal citizen there. His name was Gandy. He was a photographer and he saw this crowd and he thought he would stop these young people smashing the lamps. When he saw the multitude there, he very soon popped back indoors again. He lived next door to where the Hampshire Club is now [1971] and he watched the mob go by. Well then they thought they would pay the City Surveyor a call. He lived in Edgar Road, almost on the corner. Well he wasn't about, and I think they treated his windows the same. Then there was an amusing incident as the parade went down the street. A lone policeman came up, known as 'Sailor Jack', and he thought, 'Hello, there's a case here, glass going. We'll get these boys!' But when he saw the mob he disappeared. Seemed to vanish. Where he went to I don't know. I might say that all this time I was in the van. I was in the front so I had a good view of all that was going on.

Well then they turned down Lansdowne Avenue, a little bit downhill you see and with trees. The gun carriage ran away. It had no brakes on it of course and poor old Joe was thrown to the ground. The gun carriage collided with a tree. I saw that scar on the tree for years and years after and I thought to myself well, that is one of the results of the riot. Then they turned into St Cross Road and up Kingsgate Street smashing everything as they went. All the lamps – that always seemed to be the prize thing. Then they got to the corner of College Street. I lived on the corner of College Street then, and we had a lot of glass there on two sides of the building and I thought, 'Hello, this is going west.' However, they seemed to go past that and they went to Wolvesey Palace where they were preparing for the Winchester National Pageant which was being held on 25 June and the five following days. They went down and busted as many things up as they could. They didn't break the grand piano, but they handled it pretty roughly I think. Somebody said they tried to burn down the grandstand. Well I don't think they did, because if they had wanted to it would have gone up like a torch. Being a Boy Scout I could have done it with one match. But they picked up one piece of apparatus there – an early Saxon chariot. I thought well this is a how-do-you-do because I'm in the pageant myself. I'm a Saxon boy and now they have taken away a bit of our apparatus. However I joined in with the others and watched what was going on. They eventually got this chariot down to the bottom of the High Street and threw it over the wall into the Weirs where it rested for a good number of days. On the return of the mob from the Palace, some went the way of the Weirs[14], some went the way of College Street. It was getting a bit late, and I went the

Tuesday 26 May 1908 – the day after the Gun Riots. According to the Hampshire Chronicle, *'There was quite a pilgrimage to the gun which lay on the hard road by the side of the carriage'. (HRO 41M93/47/9)*

way of College Street and as I got to the house where I lived I thought, 'Well I think I've seen most of it.' I was getting rather tired so I went indoors out of it.

Well now that is the rough story of what happened. A good many versions have been written but being an eye witness from the start to the finish and being in the van as it were that was more or less what happened. I don't say I threw many bricks but there was plenty about to be thrown. The next day, they were going to try a repetition or something or other, but the authorities enrolled most of the ring leaders as Special Constables. That put them out of action. And they called in numbers of police from areas around, so they called the next evening's programme to a halt.

Austin Laverty, born 1896

I was in that riot. They arrested two or three people and had them down the police station. We was trying to break the police doors down and I was the one in front trying to do a bit of damage. Somebody threw a brick and hit me on the back of the head. Some time later someone said, 'Do you know your head's bleeding?' I never noticed it. It wasn't too bad. Just made a bit of a mess. Anyway it all went off all right. It just goes to show how people can get upset, however quiet they are most of the time. The authorities couldn't do anything but let it blow over. Could they tell who broke this lamp or who broke that window? Could they tell who broke the mayor's windows? Everybody had a go if they could find something to break them with.

Richard Pearce, born 1893

A Visit by King George and Queen Mary in 1912

In 1912 it must have been, when King George and Queen Mary came after the Coronation. They had a dais in the Broadway. I couldn't have been more than four and it was scorching hot. People were fainting and shopkeepers were bringing out jugs of water and glasses and giving them to the people stood there. There was a great feeling of patriotism in those days, even more so in the Brooks. It's extraordinary really. These people who were so poor, living in such appalling conditions, were all so patriotic and they almost worshipped the royalty. They were brainwashed I should think.

William Blackman, born 1908

A Visit by the Prince of Wales in 1923

When the Prince of Wales came down to open the Airlie Road estate, I was working down Christchurch Road way – I was apprentice at the time – and Mr Fennell my boss came and said, 'You don't have to work this afternoon. You can have the afternoon off.' I was supposed to have gone out of duty to see the Prince of Wales but I thought, 'Blow the Prince of Wales! I'm not interested in him'. So I went home and cleaned my bicycle all the afternoon. My wife (that is now, but before I knew her) was chasing the Prince of Wales all over the city with all the other girls. Fancy missing an opportunity like that to clean a bicycle when there was all those girls all over the place! It shows how stupid youngsters can be.

Ernest Woolford, born 1904

The visit of King George V and Queen Mary in July 1912. The King inspects veterans on his

way to the Guildhall. (HCLS)

When the Prince of Wales came, I was at All Saints School. All we children, plus children from all the other schools in Winchester met on the site where Stanmore School was going to be built, for the ceremony of Beating the Bounds. Each child had a bundle of twigs and in line astern walked around the perimeter beating the ground as we went along. The highlight of all this was our royal visitor, and we were all excited as the rest of the day was a holiday for us.

Irene Underwood, née Clewer, 1916

A Visit from King George VI and Queen Elizabeth in 1946

I think one of the most enjoyable royal functions was when Alderman Sankey was mayor and King George and Queen Elizabeth came here. That was a really enjoyable day. Alderman Sankey was a Labour member of the council, but I remember him coming in here at the *Hampshire Chronicle* waving a letter from the Palace saying that the King and Queen were coming to the College and doubtless he would like to receive them in a civic manner. He held his hand up with the letter and said, 'I don't care what it costs. I'm going to have a grand do.'

And he did. He was a very ebullient character. I think he was one of the best mayors that we've had. He was like so many people – one of the old guard of the Labour Party who, when they get older, become more Right than the Right but wouldn't admit it.

Monica Woodhouse, née Stroud, 1911

Eton Match and Domum

I always used to go to Eton match when I was young. Everybody went to Eton match, dressed up in their best clothes.

Gertrude Asher, née Whittier, 1880

In the olden days Jacob and Johnson's would put the score up every hour. If the boys beat Eton when they were playing away, you'd get anything up to two hundred people at the station to meet them and they'd carry the boys right down to the Porter's entrance shoulder high, all down the High Street cheering and clapping. And when *Domum*[15] was sung we always used to go on St Giles Hill to see a magnificent display of fireworks from up there.

Reginld O'Neill, born c. 1903

CHAPTER 3
Life in the Backstreets

The Square

On the corner of the Square was Chalkley's. Old Chalkley was a taxidermist. He was quite skilled and in those days any freak of nature like a white sparrow, a speckled blackbird or a rare bird was shot down and taken to Chalkley's for setting up.

William H.C. Blake, born 1905

When we came out of St Lawrence's after getting married in 1925, I remember Mr Chalkley who kept the shop at the top of the Square with all the fishing tackle and stuff. He came out and congratulated us. He used to know my father very well because they were both pianists and had a lot in common.

Some people who had shops in the High Street used to live at the back of them and have their private entrance in the Square. I can remember the shops in the Square in about 1912. At the bottom was a pawn shop, with three balls hanging outside, which people used to use in those days frequently on Mondays to pawn the clothes for the week. The Loke family had a cycle shop next door to us. Then there were the Poynters who were basket-makers. Next to them was an old second-hand shop. Daisy Whiting used to keep that and she always used to call us children in and say, 'Would you like a piece of Auntie Daisy's cake?' So we used to go in and she had a huge cake dish with an enormous home-made cake on it and she used to cut us off a slice. We thought she was marvellous.

We lived at number twenty-eight which was my grandmother's house and shop in the Square. She was a widow then. My grandfather had been apprenticed to an umbrella maker and he had set up there about 1850. My father was born in that house and so was I and so was my son. Grandfather used to make and mend umbrellas and Grandmother, who was a good seamstress, used to do all the sewing involved in making ladies' parasols and covers for the umbrellas. After a time though they used to send the umbrellas to Fox's in London to be repaired and then they just sold them. In slack times my grandfather used to do chair caning and china riveting as a sideline. My mother lived there and carried on the umbrella shop until she died in 1970.

Lilian Woolford, née Hibberd, 1907

Telegraphic Address—"CHALKLEY, WINCHESTER."

W. CHALKLEY'S

Sportsmen's and Naturalists' Depot,

THE SQUARE, WINCHESTER.

Every requisite (of the Best Quality) for FISHING, SHOOTING, SKATING,
AND NATURAL HISTORY.

CARTRIDGES OF EVERY DESCRIPTION AT STORE PRICES.

GUNS for SALE or HIRE.

REPAIRS executed with economy and despatch. CUTLERY Ground and Repaired
by Experienced Workmen.

TROUT FISHING TO LET by Day, Week, Month, or Season.

Warren's Winchester Directory, 1906.

Provision of Food and other Necessities

Opposite to where I lived in Chesil Street there was a big grocer's shop and I used to love to see the grocers come out and go down the cellar about two doors up, and bring up the cheeses and roll them along the pavement into the shop. You might think they would get damaged but you know cheeses in those days had a very hard rind. They were covered with cheesecloth which the bookbinder calls 'mull' and the butcher he calls it 'mutton cloth'. An old lady used to come into that shop and I don't think she hardly ever paid for anything she had. I was in there one day and Mr Kelsey who was a very gentlemanly sort of man said, 'Well Mrs Cook, you can't have any more until you've paid for some.' Well then she used to tell the tale and get away with it. She was a typical old body of the time, with a bonnet and a bodice and a skirt right down to the ground and a little red tip to her nose. They used to say that gin might have been the cause of that. She was a notorious person. Poor Mr Kelsey used to have to supply her with food. The road there was no wider than what Parchment Street is now.

Austin Laverty, born 1896

Food was cheap and we used to get criers round with everything. They used to come round the streets at night time with hot faggots and fried fish. Huge pieces for a penny. And Yarmouth bloaters. Old ladies used to come round with those. Shrimps and cockles and all sorts brought round to the door – all ready to eat.

Gertrude Asher, née Whittier, 1880

My mother used to send me along to Osmond's, a pork butcher in Hyde Street to buy faggots. They were a penny each or two for three ha'pence.

Stanley Richardson, born 1906

There used to be a large number of bakehouses here. Bakers had a pretty hard day. Bake the bread in the morning and take it out and sell it themselves. Then make the dough for the next day. There was one in Canon Street called the Wykeham bakery and there was another one up St Swithun Street next to our workshop, and then on the corner of College Street there was another with two large ovens and a smaller one. They used to heat the oven with these bundles of wood which they called faggots, and they would burn all the way and just leave the ash. Then, in about an hour, they'd open the oven door and flick it about with a wet sack on a pole and level off the embers, whatever there was left. Then in with the bread. It went straight on the brick. I used to go in there and weigh the dough. Lovely job that was weighing the dough. I always remember it was two pounds and two ounces for a two pound loaf. Two ounces for evaporation. There was another baker in Chesil Street. He wasn't our own personal

'Laverty's Corner' at the junction of Kingsgate Street and College Street before the building was demolished in 1934. Austin Laverty was relieved that its windows were not smashed during the Gun Riots when he passed by with the mob on the evening of 25 May 1908. (HCLS)

baker but I used to get a loaf there occasionally. Once when I did, and when I was having my tea I said to my mother, 'There's a potato in this slice of bread.' She said, 'That's what they do now but that one hasn't been properly processed. They boil the potatoes and when they're cold they powder them up and mix it with the bread.' It was commonplace in those days, and I'm talking now about the beginning of the Boer War. Some bakers used to put more potatoes in the bread than the others and this must have been one of them.

Austin Laverty, born 1896

Before the first war, I could get a pint of beer, a top of loaf and cheese, half ounce of baccer and a box of matches and I would put a sixpence down and I had a ha'penny change. Truth! Half ounce of Blackman cost three ha'pence. Your pint of beer was tuppence. Now, if you went in for a half ounce of baccer you had a box of matches give with it. The bread and cheese was tuppence and enough for a navvy.

Arthur W. Hodges, born 1888

A couple of doors up from my grandmother's house in Wales Street, there was a lady that had a shop in her front room. It was called Edie's shop. You went in the front door and instead of a wall being there, there was a counter. It was bare boards and these little wooden racks around the walls packed out with tins and things. She had baskets with bread in and butter and cheese under a glass dome. It was so tiny but everyone went to Edie's who lived in that area. It went for years, probably up until the late fifties. You

could walk down her back garden straight on to the river. She had a little jetty there.

Annette Hawkins, née Gough, 1949

A Survey of Housing Conditions in 1947

When I arrived in Winchester in 1947 I was amazed at the low standard that existed at that time in the heart of the city. The nearest I'd ever got to a place like it was from reading Dickens. With regard to housing, the standard was in some cases much lower than the worst type of houses I knew to exist in Liverpool. For example there were many back-to-back houses where there was no through ventilation whatsoever. The only means of access was through the front door which meant that when the dustman called and the family were dining in the front living room, he would be bringing all the putrescible matter through while they were eating.

One row of houses which still exists [1981] in Colebrook Street has no fire walls – so you can go into the roof of the first house and make your way through to the last. In these houses the living room is tiny and behind it is another smaller room, about seven feet by eight. You open the back door and go into the yard. Across the yard is the scullery. Sanitation consists of a water closet situated in an outbuilding usually at the bottom of the yard. The staircase going up to two tiny bedrooms is steep, winding and narrow. The ceilings of the living room are no more than six feet in height. This is a good example of the low standard of the houses in 1947 and, I would say, of around about 1,400 houses when I came here. These were mainly in the Brooks area but it

W. HOGAN & BROS.,

12, ST. GEORGE'S STREET,

𝕵𝖔𝖇𝖒𝖆𝖘𝖙𝖊𝖗𝖘.

HUNTERS, HACKS, AND HARNESS HORSES FOR HIRE.

Horses Broken to Ride or Drive.

RIDING LESSONS A SPECIALITY.

TERMS MODERATE.

Warren's Winchester Directory, 1906.

spread out to certain little spots outside the railway station [Chesil] where there is now a car park. One mass of little slums.

In the central car park area [Brooks], conditions absolutely beggared description. Opposite the *Echo* Office there was a stable. This belonged to a man named Hogan and he kept hacking horses there as well as about twelve sows which always had a lot of young pigs round them. The noise was terrific. With that went the objectionable smell, especially having regard to a grocer's shop which was across the road – the International Stores. From a public health point of view that was the worst place to have such an establishment. Next door to Hogan's stables going north were two houses which were within the curtilage of two slaughterhouses and I recall when I visited them for the first time, seeing children looking from their bedroom windows and seeing animals being slaughtered and

dressed. The slaughterhouses would still be doing this after ten o' clock at night. Going down St George's Street there was another slaughterhouse occupied by a local butcher called Elkington and I recall seeing the blood running down the gutters. I think there were five slaughterhouses in all.

At the back of the Queen's Head public house there was a door which was being opened and shut quite a lot during my short stay. It aroused my curiosity. The manager seemed reluctant to let me through but as Chief Environmental Health Officer I had the authority so I went in. It was a long narrow building which I discovered was a lodging house with about twelve beds either side, and buckets about eight feet apart used for urinating. Between each bed there were sacks on a piece of string dividing them.

Further along Upper Brook Street was another lodging house occupied by an Italian family. Here I got the shock of my

View of the Brooks taken from Lower Brook Street. Holy Trinity Church can be seen in the

distance, c. 1956. (HRO W/C5/10/23)

life. It was a lovely old house and could almost have been a Listed Building, but it had been allowed to become a ruin. When we went into what had been the lounge perhaps fifty years previously, we found bare boards, plaster crumbling off the walls and every so much apart there were empty paint tins on which they had placed planks to form a half circle round a fire. There was a spit with a big kettle boiling away and round this, sitting on these forms, were old ladies smoking clay pipes and men, we found out later, who had been discharged from prison. They were either drinking something or smoking something. No conversation at all. Later as we went from room to room we found the situation was repeated exactly as we had found it in the lodging house behind the Queen's Head. I would say that the situation was really worse than that at the Queen's Head. Later, the police contacted me and asked if I would go round with one of the senior detectives at twelve o' clock at night, which I did. He was after some people who had escaped from prison. He was lifting the sheets up, looking at them and then putting the sheets back again. Some of them were drunk beyond recovery. That was a horrible experience.

Further along Upper Brook Street there was a row of houses up a passage. Here I found twelve houses where the water closet was outside at right angles to the front door. Of the twelve houses I would say that only four or five had doors to them. So I would assume that if the lady of the house was in the water closet and the postman was delivering a letter, he would have to hand it to her there. This pattern was repeated in various places.

Ernest Seymour

Other Public Health Matters

Where Monks Road and Nuns Road are, there was a sloping bit of water meadow and they filled it up with garbage from all the dustcarts and so on. They put the houses on top of the old garbage and tins and everything. Within a few years some of the ground there sunk six foot. Eventually they had to pull one of the end houses down, but for over twenty years the sewerage used to come over the top of the pan in four of the houses and run over into the river where the animals used to drink. The sewerage from the big houses at Abbotts Barton ran straight into the river there too. We had any amount of people dying of tuberculosis in those days. What they used to call bovine TB but it was in pigs too. There were pigs with big fat 'eads. Hundreds and hundreds of cows got slaughtered because they had TB. Things got cleaned up and it stopped a lot of the consumption, but that had to wait until after the second war. And you'll hardly credit that until after that war too they still had bucket sanitation at St John's – right close to the Guildhall.

Reginald Best, born 1897

Self-help in case of Sickness

The best way you could get a doctor was at the Winchester Provident Dispensary in the Square. That was going ever since I can remember. There were five or six doctors who had their different days and different times in there. You paid in sixpence a week, and if you needed to see a doctor you would go up there and he used to make up your prescription straight away. But for a doctor, and so much [money] if they were ill, most men if they could possibly do so used to join a club. There were

1931

WINCHESTER PROVIDENT DISPENSARY.

No. *99*

Name *Walsh C.*

Address *111 Egbert Road*

	s	d	Fines		s	d	Fines
July	1	6	1	Jan.			
Aug.	1	6		Feb.			
Sept.	1	6		Mar.			
Oct.	1	6		Apl.			
Nov.	1	6		May			
Dec.	1	6		June			

All Payments must be paid in advance at the Dispensary, on the First Tuesday of every Month, at 6 p.m. Payments may be made on the evening of any subsequent Tuesday, but a Fine of One Penny will be imposed.

F. C. MALLETT, *Secretary.*

Medical Attendant :—

MR. E. H. V. HENSLEY.

*Days of Attendance:—*Monday & Thursday, 2.30 p.m.

The Dispenser attends at the Dispensary daily at 2.30 p.m. and 6.30 p.m., except on Wednesday at 5 to 5.45 p.m. only.

RULES.

1.—Sick Members must, when able, attend at the Dispensary at the appointed time.

2.—Sick Members requiring attendance at their homes, must send this card to the house of the Medical Attendant by nine o'clock in the morning.

3.—No application is to be made by Members for attendance at their homes on Sundays, or after nine o'clock in the morning, except in cases of accident, or sudden illness.

4.—Two Pence will be charged for each bottle, to be repaid when the bottle is returned.

5.—Members in arrear with their Subscriptions are not entitled to Medical Attendance or Medicines.

6.—A fine of One Penny will be demanded for each month in arrear.

No Medical Advice or Medicine can be obtained at the Dispensary unless this Card is produced.

Winchester Provident Dispensary membership card. (HRO 65M90W/11)

different sorts of clubs like the Oddfellows or the Foresters and you paid so much a month and you had your doctor and you had your medicine and so much a week if you were ill. My mother put me in the Oddfellows as a juvenile, and from a juvenile I went right the way through and I'm still an Oddfellow now. That's how they safeguarded theirselves in the way of illness. If a man was ill he got sixteen shillings a week this way, and very often it was more than he earned when he was well. Hundreds and hundreds of people belonged.

Richard Pearce, born 1893

Life in the Brooks

Middle Brook Street at that time consisted of appalling slum property. There was a riding stable, belonging to Mr Hogan, with the smell of horses and manure. Nearby was a rag and bone store which gave off a terrible stench. In spite of the poverty, there were several public houses where, presumably, the poor people went to drown their sorrows, thereby making themselves even poorer.

There were swarms of rats and the cottages were infested with fleas and bedbugs. I don't remember coming from Middle Brook Street to here in Lower Brook, but when we came here we would have had no floor coverings. It would have been bare boards throughout the house. For a hearthrug we'd probably have an old chaff sack, something like that and the furniture was absolutely squalid. Over the back of our house they kept pigs and there were chickens everywhere.

I believe the parish priests did what they

could, but the situation was quite impossible to alleviate. In my early life I never saw anything of the cathedral clergy who were then living in the large houses in the Close with several servants. It seemed to be, '... you Jack I'm all right'. Somewhere I once read, 'In any of the cities of Europe, one can find the clergy living on the sunny side of the cathedral, whilst one finds all the slums and vice and brothels where the shadow of the great cathedral falls.' This was most certainly so in Winchester in the early part of this century.

Families were often huge. One of our next door neighbours had seventeen children whilst our other had thirteen. Such numbers of children in a family were common. There was a great community spirit and people helped each other, something which doesn't exist much today. I remember going to the Mission Hall in Silver Hill. It didn't seem to matter there how shabby we were. We would attend the various denominations for a while if there was an outing in the near future, and I remember going to the Salvation Army and the various churches. Although we were mostly Church of England we got a much warmer welcome elsewhere. The C of E churches seemed to favour the better-off people.

William Blackman, born 1908

There were no indoor toilets at all. They were right outside in the yard, so it was awful if it was wet and you had to run up the passageway and round the back of the house to go. It was horrible. When you opened the old wooden door, in front of you was this wooden seat going the width of the toilet. That's all there was in there. Just a seat with a cistern high up with a chain you pulled to make it flush. It was very cold and bleak and you can just imagine in the winter time having to go out and sit in there. It was dreadful. Really dreadful. Even at school the toilets were like it. We didn't know any better then though. Of course there wasn't any toilet paper in those days either. We had to cut up newspaper to use. That was all strung up on a string that hung on the wall. The *Radio Times* was the thing when radio came in. They were the best thing to use and were very prominent in people's toilets.

Joan Halford, née Edmonds, 1926

My parents were living in Middle Brook Street when my father died in February 1908. I was born on 1 June in the same year. He came home from the Royal Hotel where he worked as a sort of cabman driving a fly. My mother said that sometimes he would take a sort of wagonette with seats all round to Warsash for crab teas and that sort of thing.

Then one morning he went to work and – this is what my mother always said – he came home about nine which was most unusual and she said, 'What have you come home for Will?' and he said, 'I've come home to die my dear. I don't want to die but I know I'm dying'. She laid him down on the couch and before they got a doctor to him he was dead. He knew, he knew. There was absolutely nothing to even bury my father but his employer at the Royal Hotel took charge of that and paid the undertaker. And there were seven children and me unborn.

Well, my brother John went away to an orphanage the day I was born. He was ten. They took him to the station, tied a label on him, put him in the charge of the guard and he went down somewhere in Somerset – on the very day I was born. My mother never saw him until he came back eight years later, which was the first time I had ever seen him. It must have been terrible times for my mother. She loved her children.

My sister Rose, she went to an orphanage in Southampton, and soon afterwards my brother Fred worked for a fish shop. My brother George went to an aunt in Fleet. My eldest sister Lucy was twelve and a half and she went out to work. Nelly was a bit younger than her and she stayed home to look after me and my brother Jim who was just a bit older than me. They used to take me up to where my mother worked at the old God Begot. That was a hotel then, a posh hotel, and they used to take me up when it was necessary for her to breast feed me.

If my mother had gone pleading she could have probably obtained more assistance. She had been born a farmer's daughter and for her time was much better educated than many of her neighbours. She did apply once for some charity and attended a meeting at the Guildhall, presided over by the mayor who said he felt her case didn't warrant help, and she came away empty-handed. I fancy she didn't grovel. There couldn't have been a more deserving case.

William Blackman, born 1908

I didn't like it, but another thing I had to do sometimes was collecting rents in the Brooks. There were some dreadful places down there and they belonged to St John's Charity. You went down a kind of tunnel and it opened out into a sort of court and the lavatories were in full view of everyone. The houses always suffered from the frost cracking them in the winter. Some of the rents were as low as three shillings a week. These old girls there were very pleasant and we had very few defaulters. They always used to offer a cup of tea which I didn't like to take.

William H.C. Blake, born 1905

If we wanted a bath there was always a zinc one hung up outside on the wall. We would have to have the bath in the scullery but it was warm in there because of the fire underneath the copper. We didn't have many baths though. Not that we were dirty. It was just that it was such a performance to have one.

Granny used to sit me on the table with a big bowl of hot water and wash me all over from top to toe. Give me a good wash every day rather than have baths. I can't ever recall having a bath at Granny's and I didn't have many when I was in Colebrook Street until I was earning myself and then, with my sixpence, I would go to the public baths by the cathedral once a week. We just had to keep clean by washing ourselves down daily because baths in the houses didn't come in until long after the war.

I remember my uncles when they came home from work, they didn't have baths in the house either. Especially on Saturday, their half-day, they would go down to the bottom of Lower Brook where there were some public baths. They would go in there for sixpence a time. As soon as they went in they would give their trousers to the lady outside and she would give them to a little girl who would run up to Middle Brook and give them to her mother. Then she would sponge the trousers down and sort of clean them and press them all for two pence. Then the little girl would run back with

Wharf Hill showing the Dog and Duck in the early twentieth century. One of five pubs within close proximity, it lost its licence in 1923 and was demolished in 1937.

them in time for when they'd finished their baths to have the trousers to put on nice and clean and pressed. Then they would go off and see their young ladies.

I always used to know when Uncle Vic was in the baths because he used to sing at the top of his voice. The only time I ever heard him sing was when he was in the bath. A crowd of us kids on a Saturday afternoon used to have great fun listening to the men in the baths. You could tell who was in there by the way they were singing.

Joan Halford, née Edmonds, 1926

My mother-in-law had the pub called the Queen's Head and also what they called in those days a lodging house for casuals – people on the road. They used to spend sixpence for a night's bed and breakfast. The beds were round the back above the stables where the grooms would have been years ago. I will say this for my mother-in-law, she used to put clean sheets on. She used to buy bales of twill and cut them and make sheets. And she employed a lady to come round each day and make up the beds. She was good in that respect. They had a clean bed. The big house opposite which is now *The Echo* was a lodging house as well. We lived two doors up from the Queen's Head in Piper's old house that had been a mineral water factory. In between was a slaughterhouse that belonged to Kaine's, the pork butcher. We were in among the slaughterhouses. On Mondays when they had the cattle market they used to drive the animals down the road. Make 'em run, you know. Then all Monday night we got no sleep because the cows were mooing and the sheep were bleating and everything was making a noise all night. Well the next day all we heard was bang, bang. They were shooting them.

Louisa Lewis, née Salter, 1918

The Brooks church was the Anglo-Catholic church of Holy Trinity where the standard of music was very high, and it was well attended. One organist, Dr Cyril Fogwell, is honoured by a memorial in St Sepulchre's in Holborn. He was organist for twenty-six years but sadly died fairly young. He was for a while assistant organist in the cathedral. Gordon Beasley, one of the choirboys of Holy Trinity, became a distinguished musician in Cape Town. He was born in a cottage opposite the Parish Hall in Upper Brook Street. He had no opportunities for help in his career and was almost self-taught. A Reverend John Mace[16] was rector for many years and the church was packed for his funeral service. Some of the women of the Brooks attended wearing their white aprons.

William Blackman, born 1908

St John's Street

St John's Street where I used to live – that was a lovely little street. They used to call it Incubator Street because all the women had so many children, and they used to sit outside and nurse their babies. Suckle 'em. And nobody used to walk by and take a bit of notice of 'em.

Ernest Woolford, born 1904

Wharf Hill, Water Lane and Wales Street

This town hasn't always been prosperous by a long way. They were all working class at one time down places like Water Lane and Wales Street. Hard to tell how people survived, especially with some of these little old houses where there were eight or nine children in a two-bedroomed house. Or one bedroom, some of them. I know where the missis' mother lived, opposite the mill in Wharf Hill – they only had one bedroom there and a landing. There was six of them and there had been twins as well who'd died. I don't know where they slept. There was only one room downstairs. One up and one down. How the devil they used to sleep, I don't know. Must have been one on top of the other.

I never had nothing when I got married. I never had any money hardly at all. I just had enough to get a bit of furniture together, and when I got married what did they do? One of my brothers-in-law belonged to a band in Winchester. He got half the band come down. Another one goes up the boozer and brings down the beer. There's one made the sandwiches and another one made something else. That was our wedding breakfast. That was down Wharf Hill. That was where the band was. There must have been forty or fifty houses round there then. They haven't half pulled a lot down. We had a good old sing song, a proper old jamboree down there. Well that's what they used to do. All work together. The working class all mucked together. If one was down they looked after the one who was down. Today if one's down they tread on top of them.

Victor Gough, born 1908

Wales Street early in the twentieth century. (WMS)

Canon Street

Canon Street used to be a very rough place. They used to call it Big Gun Street.

Arthur W. Hodges, born 1888

The Canon Street area was harum-scarum. Now its la-di-da. We were afraid to go down there. There were such a lot of ragged urchins. They said it was Three Pubs, Three Brothels Street. The sailors used to come up from Portsmouth to visit Canon Street I've been told.

Lilian Woolford, née Hibberd, 1907

In number sixty-three there was a family in every room. They all had a kitchen range and that's what they had to do everything on. There would be napkins steaming three or four deep all round the fireguards. Number sixty-four was a much bigger house and was let off in nice apartments. That's where we lived before we moved to St Swithun's Terrace. I didn't interfere with anyone in Canon Street and no-one interfered with me.

Louisa Lewis, née Salter, 1918

Some of these houses were lovely inside if only people could discover what lay behind twelve layers of wallpaper – and that was oak panelling. They never removed the paper because it made the houses warmer. Near the junction with Southgate Street was a pub. On Friday nights, soldiers would frequent it and then they would wander

across the road. Here there were two houses which I discovered in a survey had been painted with life-size ladies. An old lady told me she remembered when the soldiers, half-drunk, used to be invited in, taken upstairs and were very soon without a penny in their pockets. Whoever painted those pictures was some artist!

Ernest Seymour

Eviction, Debt, Unemployment and Trade Union Activity

In those days people were always in trouble owing rent. I can remember, about 1911, old Granny Bunce had been turned out of her house right opposite St John's church. The bailiffs came and threw all her furniture out

12-18 Water Lane taken from St John's churchyard, c. 1956. (HRO W/C5/10/23)

1-7 Canon Street, c. 1956. (HRO W/C5/10/23)

11-20 Canon Street, c. 1956. (HRO W/C5/10/23)

in the middle of the road in the pouring rain and she went up and down the street crying. My old granny took her in for the night but she said, 'I can't keep you here. I can't afford it so you'll have to go up the workhouse.' It was wicked there. The old men used to stand round the stove drying tea leaves to smoke and the old workhouse master used to come round and say, 'Come on! I want you to break some coal up' and all that. We got into debt ourselves. There was a milkman called Mr Elkins who had a place up in Morn Hill. My father asked him if we could have a week's milk on tick and he said, 'No Mr Woolford you can't. If you can't pay this week, you won't be able to pay next week, or the week after'.

My father told me once he'd been thirteen pounds in debt. He'd just got the last bit paid off and then he got out of work again. Got the sack, or stood off as they called it. Heartbreaking. Then sometimes he got 'frozen out'. This was when it was so cold they couldn't do any work and they got no pay. Nothing. In those days, Winnall Moors got frozen over. Then my father would go down there taking all the chairs from the house, and some skates he'd bought second-hand from the pawn shop and make a bit of money hiring them out. He used to mend all us kids' shoes – snob 'em. He was always at work. Amazing man.

He came back from the first war even more of a rebel than he was before. He'd been born and lived in London, and came to Winchester to help build Winchester Barracks after it caught fire[17]. In 1919 he joined the Labour Party and he became Secretary of the Union of Building Trade Operatives. And that's all you used to get. You had it for breakfast. You had it lunch time. You had it tea time. You had it for supper time. Nothing but politics. He was absolutely sold on it. In 1920, we had our first May Day procession and my father made quite a rousing speech on a coal cart against the gun near King Alfred. The working class used to boo him every time he got up and spoke, but he lived that down eventually. A lot of people weren't trade union inclined and I think my father was probably twenty years in advance of his time. In 1924 we had the building strike (which was actually a lock-out) which I joined. My father was still the secretary. Every single bricklayer and every labourer and almost every carpenter came out on strike. Seven weeks we were out.

The chief difference between when I was young and now is that times are better. The poverty was dreadful. There was so much unemployment before the First World War. My father lived in abject poverty. It was terrible days believe me. It was cruel. Really cruel.

Ernest Woolford, born 1904

Charity

When I was a boy and my father was out of work, there was no money coming in. Nothing. So we used to go to the soup kitchen. We used to be allowanced out with two slices of bread and margarine each. The choirmaster had two sisters who were pretty well off, and they used to give us perhaps a dozen tickets worth a penny each to go to the soup kitchen in Water Lane, where you could get a bowl of soup. You sat along the bench – all the boys and girls used to do it – or you could go and get a pennyworth of soup and bring it home. It was organized by local charitable people. Good people like these sisters. They used to buy the tickets off somebody and they would distribute them to the poor people. You could get a quart jug for a penny and a lump of roly-poly pudding with currants and raisins.

Ernest Woolford, born 1904

Corner of Market Street, there was a big cake shop and we used to see the children queued up there most evenings for the day before's stale bread and cakes. There were a lot of poor people in Winchester. We had some friends who were butchers. Wright their name was. On Saturday night he used to more or less give away what he had left. They were good people.

Lilian Woolford, née Hibberd, 1907

If you wanted to go into the hospital you went to the rich of the parish and got an 'In-patient' paper which cost these people two guineas. That was a red one they gave you, and you went into the hospital. If you wanted 'Out-patients' it cost these people one guinea, and that was the black paper.

O'Neill family

In 1919 I was apprenticed to a bricklayer, Mr Fennel of Fennel & Co., for five years. St John's church used to have this charity left by a gentleman by the name of Cunninghame Graham, who was a curate[18]. He left this charity for two choirboys to be apprenticed each year with a premium of twenty-five pounds each. My brother and I were both apprenticed under that scheme.

Ernest Woolford, born 1904

Relief Work for the Unemployed

There were some relief works in the park to level off the ground to try to find work for the unemployed before the First World War. You know all the steps that are on St Giles Hill and all the paths that have been cut? Well, my father was amongst those that worked on that. That was relief work too.

Ernest Woolford, born 1904

Where the recreation ground is, that was all bog one time. I remember when it was all bog and all those out of work used to have to put in so many hours down there, spreading all the rubbish and stuff to make it up, so they could get so many food vouchers. When the men ran out of dole they started on the vouchers. That was a kind of means test. They'd come round and say, 'How many sons you got? Two? Well you only want four chairs then. Get rid of the rest.' People used to know when they was coming and used to take out half the furniture from the house and put it in someone else's. Well, I've got to say that drinking was the main occupation when they had the money. It was beer then. Not made with a lot of chemicals. You could get it for threepence or fourpence a pint – as long as you'd got a shilling... well that was the idea of giving them vouchers when they sent them down the park to work.

Victor Gough, born 1908

CHAPTER 4
The First World War

The Day War broke out

I can remember the day war broke out on the fourth of August 1914. It had a very, very red sunset. That's all I can remember – this very, very red sunset and I thought, did it mean something?

Dorothy Yaldren, née Newman, 1903

Mobilization

My father was in the 1st Battalion the Rifle Brigade, stationed in Colchester, and had been loaned to the Winchester depot with other officers and NCOs to assist with the training of the Militia who had a summer camp on Morn Hill. This would have been June or July 1914. I clearly remember the regimental buglers going from street to street on the morning of the fourth of August 1914 to summon all troops to the depot as the First World War had started and mobilization was in full swing. In a matter of days, troops began to pour into Winchester to be billeted in every house and building which could be commandeered. Winchester College and most of the schools were filled with badly-dressed and very hungry soldiers. The Regular Battery of Field Artillery was

billeted in Danemark School. I remember the guns lined up on the area of grass by the school buildings.

Stanley Richardson, born 1906

Billeting of Troops in the Town

Troops were billeted in everybody's house. You had to have about three men. Put them up where you could. Anywhere. I remember we had some Surrey Yeomanry here but they were very nice gentlemen. They weren't here long. They were just getting fitted up for clothes and everything to go out to France. I worked up at the camp at Morn Hill as a secretary. There was no roads. It was all mud. I worked with a lot of girls from London. They were some real smart girls I can tell you. You know, how they were to what we were. We were brought up so modest. Oh dear oh dear! They were such lively girls.

Gertrude Asher, née Whittier, 1880

Part of father's warehouse in Lower Brook had been commandeered before the war, and they put in equipment and uniforms and that sort of thing. When the war broke out they immediately used it. The East Bucks. Regiment was stationed there but they were

Part of the military camp at Avington Park, 1918. In the earlier stages of the war, soldiers were

taken up to Morn Hill afterwards because a lot of them fell through the floor. I think forty fell through the floor. They must have been in the sheds and been too heavy for them.

Beatrice and Mildred Forder

Military Camps on the Downs

In 1914 I went to Cheesefoot Head when the 27th Division was made up, and I sees King George[19] up there. He reviewed them troops on Cheesefoot Head. It was a magnificent view to see 'em all go by, not thinking that before long three parts of them would be gone. I was on me own when I see 'em go along the

Petersfield Road in front of King George. I stood on a bank and took me hat off and waved, and he waved back. I never see such a sight. Not long afterwards they marched and it was a shocking day. It rained in torrents all the while when they went from 'ere to Southampton. Some of them was back here not long after. Wounded. They'd got cut to pieces. When you come to think about it – what a beautiful lot of men!

Arthur W. Hodges, born 1888

We remember the Alresford Road being packed with mules and carts and steam engines, from as far as you could see and down

60

under canvas. (IWM Q30106/7)

to the Broadway – taking materials to these camps at Morn Hill and Winnall and Avington. Sometimes they just used to go so far and then they couldn't move because they got stuck in the mud. They brought all these men over from India in bitter weather clad just in their white shorts. They used to stay all along this road, shivering. People used to go out with jugs of cocoa or bring them in, poor men. They brought over the Argyll and Sutherland Highlanders from India in the middle of winter in their kilts. They marched up this road and they must have lost half of them before they got to camp. They just collapsed. They used to suffer from what they called the ague[20]. It was a terrible time. Then, towards the end of the war, it would be one

mass of black troops coming along. A few regiments of them were stationed up the hill. We used to have them in and give them a meal. Everyone did. We used to have them down of an evening.

O'Neill family

All over the downs around Winchester they had camps of tremendous numbers of soldiers from all over the world – Indians, Americans, Canadians. A great number died simply of exposure up there in the winter because of lying out in the rain and the snow and slush. There was so much mud up there. I can remember going up there where these poor wretches were encamped and often they would come and ask if they could sleep on the floor down in the town, in the houses, and most of the Brooks people I think in those days would let them. I know my mother did. She let half a dozen come and sleep and I expect she gave them a hot drink, though they probably didn't want anything except to sleep on the floor. To be dry. None of these people even locked their doors. Even we never did because there was never any muggings or break-ins. Anyway, there wasn't much to break in for. When we woke in the mornings they'd be gone because they had to get back for reveille.

William Blackman, born 1908

At the end of the war they built this branch line to Morn Hill camp from off the Newbury line that ran along the end of our garden. We saw the steam trains branch off and go right up through Harry Walters' fields taking food and stores. The old thing used to chuff away. It was all up hill. It had to pull hard to get up there. They had American troops working on the line. Darkies mainly. They were very good workers, and as happy as you like. They'd be singing away all the time. Everything was done with a pick and shovel in them days. No digging machines. They used to come down in skips loaded with chalk on this little light railway. The track was about two foot to two foot six wide, and it was in little sections that they slotted together like a kid's railway set. They used to come belting down and for a brake all they had was a piece of wood rammed in between the frame of the skip and the wheel. Sometimes the wood

Black American troops in 1918, constructing a railway which linked the military camps with the Didcot Newbury Southampton railway line from a point just north of Winchester. (IWM Q31221)

would slip out or it would break. Then they'd jump off and shout out, 'Look out below! Oy oy below there! Coming down! Whoooa!' and everyone would run for their lives. Off it would go down to the bottom and then they had the bother of picking it all up again. Us kids thought it was great fun to watch. They thought it was real good fun too.

Ben Kerley, born 1909

War Profiteers

The dealers used to crawl around the camps seeing what they could get. One day one of them came to me and said, 'I've got something that would interest you Best. Come down and look at my store in Water Lane.' And do you know that in this store he'd got all the shoes we'd made for the Royal Garrison Artillery to take to France? He'd got them off a farrier sergeant who couldn't be bothered to pack them and take them over to France. We'd had a whole lot of big horses come in for us to take their measurements, and we'd taken a lot of trouble with 'em. Some horses have got a foot like a maple leaf, some as we used to say were like an apple dumpling and some were like a mule. We made all the shoes a purpose for them, stamped 'W. Best, Winchester' underneath them and sold them to the government for twenty-five pounds. You'd never credit another farrier got 'em and made any amount of money putting 'em on.

Reginald Best, born 1897

Riots, Fights, Drunkenness and Protest

I recall the riots in the 1914-1918 war. The Welsh were the worst. They attacked the police station in the Broadway, smashed all the windows and tried to get out one of the Welshmen who had been arrested. But they were beaten off, or held back by the police, and then the Rifle Brigade from the depot marched down the High Street with fixed bayonets – straight down the High Street in line abreast to clear it – and the Welsh went out one end while the Rifle Brigade came in the other. I actually saw that happen.

Stanley Richardson, born 1906

The worse lot I ever see was the Newfoundlanders. No law and order with them. Awful. One lot of trouble I see – the police arrested one of their men and I never seen it done before. They got a scaffold pole from somewhere and the men charged and broke them doors down at the police station to get their man out. They was all right if they wasn't interfered with. Now the Americans – some very nice people among them but I'll tell you what Sir, those blacks I liked them better. You could talk to them. The Yanks themselves they had too much money in both wars. When the first war finished there was a lot of Yanks in the town. They always seemed too big. They had some money to spend and that's why our chaps didn't like it because they didn't have much.

Arthur W. Hodges, born 1888

During the war we came to live in a little bungalow that was owned by Harry Walters, who had Winnall Manor Farm. My father worked for him as driver of a steam traction

Rioting soldiers in the High Street being dispersed by police[21] in 1915. (DN)

engine. The bungalow was right by the Newbury line and there was a level crossing at the end of our garden. There was a British sentry there who was meant to stop soldiers from the camp crossing the fields but he used to turn a blind eye. They were supposed to go the Alresford Road way but black and white Americans and our own boys used to come back along Wales Street after an evening in Winchester. They went down as far as the church and came round by the brick wall where the pond was. Some of them used to get wet through because they were so drunk they fell into the pond. Drunken soldiers used to knock on our door at all hours of the night. Mother used to bolt it and tell us not to make a sound because often father was away with the thrashing tackle on other farms. There were fights with knives and guns in the streets, and there was an incident at the Ship Inn in Wales Street. One night three black Americans went in and asked the landlord for beer. He said he hadn't got any beer for black men and so they said, 'That's all right landlord, cheerio', and went away. The next night they came back and put a revolver on the counter. 'Three pints please, landlord' they said. He was so frightened. He thought he was going to be killed. So he bolted out the back and sent his wife to see to them. It didn't matter about her! So she went out and said, 'What do you want boys?' and they said, 'We want some beer please ma'am'. So then it was out with the pints and everything was happy after that. No trouble at all. I suppose he got used to it in the end.

Ben Kerley, born 1909

While I'm away

My father joined the Royal Engineers under Lord Derby's Scheme[22] in 1916, and he said to me, 'Look, you're the eldest in the family. You look after your mother while I'm away.' I was twelve years old and I cried my eyes out. He didn't get any leave – any leave at all – and we didn't see him again for three and a half years.

Ernest Woolford, born 1904

A Schoolboy's War Effort

During the First World War I spent the last eighteen months of my time at school up in Mr Dyer's field here 'digging for victory'. I used to go up with the school nearly every day and plant potatoes and various things according to the season.

Reginald O'Neill, born c. 1903

Benefiting from being a Boy Scout

I joined the Withers Own in December 1918, and within a week of passing my Tenderfoot Badge I was helping to lay out newspapers, arrange tables, find cards, ludo sets and other games for the American troops returning from the war who were sent to Morn Hill camp before repatriation. This was a particularly sought-after job by the Scouts because they were often sent home with parcels of food and luxuries which at that time our mothers found impossible to buy in the shops. I well remember returning with several bottles of OK Sauce and two tins of Prince Edward cigars. The cigars were greatly appreciated by my father who had just returned after serving four years in France.

Stanley Richardson, born 1906

American troops in Bridge Street passing from camp to the Front, 1918. (IWM Q31209)

Armistice Day, 11 November 1918. Wintonians gather in the Broadway outside the Guildhall. (LL)

College Casualties

In that one house at Winchester College, Beloes (which was only founded in 1905), only eighty had reached fighting age by 1918. Thirty-nine of the eighty were killed, that sort of figure. I've got a photograph of the Corps NCOs of 1910. Eleven sergeants sitting in a row and only four of us were alive at the end.

J.W. Parr, born 1905

The Day War ended

Everybody went mad. They turned off the engine outside which made all the machines work at Warren's. We packed up and went outside in the High Street, and everybody was going crazy cheering. The College boys apparently didn't wait to get out the door. They got out of the windows if they were on the ground floor and they were on top of cars and taxis. Everybody was going wild. They were dancing down the High Street and somebody in the army grabbed hold of me. There was a whole line of us and I was caught up in it and so I had to go and we were all singing and dancing down the street. People both sides were watching the younger ones and I caught sight of my mother's face. She looked in horror at me, but I couldn't stop because I was caught in it. But it was great, it really was.

Dorothy Yaldren, née Newman, 1903

I honestly don't remember the end of that war. I do remember my mother taking me to my aunt's. They were undertakers and considerably better off than we were, and they would have had the *Telegraph*. I can remember my aunt showing me a page. They had columns and columns of the casualties and the deaths of these people over on the Western Front. It must have been about the time of the Somme. I remember that but I don't remember the end of the war.

William Blackman, born 1908

The American cemetery at Morn Hill showing the military camp in the distance, 1918. In 1920 the bodies were exhumed for re-burial in the USA. (IWM Q31252)

CHAPTER 5
Childhood, Youth and Family Life

Schooldays

My earliest memory is the day that my brother started school. He cried all day long and our school teacher stuck his face up with sticking plaster in the finish because she couldn't stand it any longer.

Ernest Woolford, born 1904

Children from Pitt could either walk from Pitt across the down to Compton, or they could walk to St Faith's. At one time Compton school was too small and didn't have room for them. Of course all the farm people used to come from the top of Stanmore Lane and Downe. People didn't take any notice of a couple of mile walk to school and back. Very often they would come in the morning and they were wet through. They used to come and sit in their clothes. Sometimes if a teacher spotted it, they used to put them in front of the fire to warm them but their clothes just used to dry on them and it didn't seem to hurt them at all.

Richard Pearce, born 1893

I loved school myself. I loved walking to it by the water along up through the Weirs. First I went to the infant school in Colebrook Street. You went there until you were six and then you went on up to what we called the Big School and we felt we'd really arrived.

I don't think people now would believe what the infant school was like. The main room was long, and in the middle under the window was the headmistress at her desk. At the bottom of the room were some stairs up to a window which was about half way up the wall. There were big crosses painted on them and that's where the children sat, on one of those crosses. All round the walls there were big slates and you had a slate pencil to draw on them with, which made a horrible squeak. We had a box of sand we used to write in with a kind of wooden pencil thing.

After I left infant school I went to the Central School in Abbey Passage. There were two entrances – one into the girls' playground and the other to the boys'. If you were late when the gates were shut at 9.00 a.m., you had to wait outside until the morning hymn was sung and then latecomers had to stand in front of the headmaster. If you had no note to say why you were late, you were caned. There were three classes on the ground floor. Two in a large room divided by a wooden partition and a small class in another room. The wide staircase was stone on which we could make a lovely noise by banging our feet down. The second floor was laid out in the same way as the ground. The divided rooms made life difficult for the teachers. They obviously could not have two singing lessons going on at the same time. In the centre of the room was a large black stove that served both classes, and had a heavy fireguard all round it. When it was very cold the teachers tried to stand as near to it as possible but we poor kids had to shiver. Some of us wore mittens if we had chilblains. If anyone cried loud enough because they were cold, they were called out to come and get a 'warm' by the fire.

I and two of my friends went in for an exam. We passed and got two pounds and a chance to go for a scholarship. What pleased us most was to see our names in the *Hampshire Chronicle*. I couldn't take up the scholarship as it would have cost two hundred pounds for college and books, and my parents didn't have even two hundred shillings. There was little chance of the working class getting anywhere if money was involved. I suppose our axioms were 'Poor but honest' and 'Cleanliness is next to Godliness'.

Dorothy Yaldren, née Newman, 1903

I first went to the Roman Catholic school which was by the recreation ground. I was only there from four to five because there wasn't room in another school. My mother wouldn't keep me there afterwards because she didn't want me to be a Roman Catholic. But I can remember while I was there two incidents. One was when a teacher chased us all out into the playground because an aeroplane went over and it was such an extraordinary thing. Yes it was about 1912. The other thing which has always vividly remained in my memory; there was a black family in Winchester at that time and this little black boy was in this class where I was. For some reason, one day the teacher held him up by his collar and just beat the daylights out of him in front of the whole class. It was obviously a complete thing of colour prejudice. They were probably the only black family in this city and if I remember their name was Peters and they lived down Eastgate Street way.

At five I went on to Holy Trinity and that was pretty grim there. The toilets were out in the yard and they were very, very rough. You know if they had one in the back of a pub today they'd be shut down. The conditions at Holy Trinity, with the masters and that, was pretty grim too. We used to go home midday for dinner, and when we got back one would be as drunk as a lord with bottles all round him. I remember too going along to the toilets many times and one of the male masters was snogging with one of the female teachers. Quite a common thing and all the kids would giggle about that. Another master got a couple of boys to take wood and coal belonging to the school out to his house in Hyde Street, but he made the mistake of beating one of them one day. The two boys went to the Guildhall and insisted on seeing the 'Eddication Officer'. The porter there scratched his head but eventually got them an interview. They really spilt the beans and the chap packed up his few things and that's the last we ever saw of him. He was finished.

The Weir, Winchester.

The Weirs, about 1910, as it looked when Dorothy Yaldren enjoyed walking along there to go to the Central School. (HCLS)

When I was twelve they had an examination to sort out the brighter boys who would go on to St Thomas's which was a slightly higher grade school. What I remember was that most of the boys didn't even try because they didn't want to leave Holy Trinity, but whether for that reason or not I went to St Thomas's. The discipline was better there but quite honestly the only thing I remembered from St Thomas's was the woodwork classes. I always remembered how to do simple carpentry. I liked that, but as for the rest of the teaching I'm afraid, well… a few years after I left, and I left at fourteen, I was really almost illiterate. But I did something about that eventually. No schooling ever did it for me. Holy Trinity School is now gone from Cossack Lane.

William Blackman, born 1908

The nurse used to come into the school sometimes to see if the children's heads were clean. If they had any lice they used to have to go to the clinic in the Square. One day I was sitting behind a girl who had long plaits. She had a parting down the middle at the back and I could see these little grey things running up and down. I sat back and asked the teacher if I could sit somewhere else.

Irene Underwood, née Clewer, 1916

The standard of food at the College was probably pretty good, but there wasn't enough of it unless you spent a good deal of money at School Shop. Tea was only bread and butter. We bought our own jam and that sort of thing or you could get a hot dish from School Shop. It was coldish by the time it

Holy Trinity School in Cossack Lane where, according to William Blackman, the conditions were 'pretty grim'. (WMS)

arrived, sent over with a plate over it. A couple of eggs or something like that if you had the money but I didn't have very much money. It wouldn't be considered adequate according to modern standards. You wouldn't dare feed an Approved School on it now [1970]. It wasn't until I was a housemaster that the housemaster provided anything other than bread and jam for tea.

J.W. Parr, born 1892

One of the things I resented strongly when I was at Winchester College, just before the Second World War, was the lack of links between the College and the city. We had essentially zero contact with the city and I felt totally cut off from all the people of my age outside the walls. We had this sort of upper-class speech and we were effectively isolated. There was absolutely no effort to reach out to the town, and relations with the Cathedral were certainly not warm.

One thing we could rebel against was the College Cadet Force, but the school treated us in a very intelligent way. They said, 'OK. No problem. Then you'd better do something useful with the time when other people are drilling.' So we had to dig in the College garden and grow vegetables. This we cheerfully did and that was our military service and we couldn't make any moral objections to that. We had a tiny little piece of land between the College and the river where we raised very sickly-looking cabbages.

Frederick Dyson, born c. 1920

Working before leaving School

Stratton's farm at Stanmore was a good source of income to me because during the school holidays I used to go up there when they were harvesting. I used to have to lead the horses from about half a dozen sheaves apart and then stop while they used to load those sheaves up onto the wagon, and then lead them on again and stop and do that again – right over until the field was cleared. When that wagon was full you used to lead the horses back to the rick, leave that wagon there and they used to unload it and bring the empty wagon back to start off again. We used to do all the field right the way up. Used to start about ten o'clock after the dew had gone off the corn, and used to work until eight o'clock at night. I got six shillings a week for that, and that was a lot of money. It was my money. My mother said, 'You earned it. You have it.' So I did, and I used to buy myself clothes and things like that. Bought myself a bike which was a good thing in those days. The men, they used to earn overtime but they never got the money then. They used to get it at Michaelmas which was the time when all the farmhands used to change if they wanted another job. Right the way up to Romsey Road and the other side as well was Stratton's farm. There was a bank at the back – where the Queen's Head is now [1969] – that used to be covered in cowslips. Everyone used to go up there in the summer time picking cowslips. It seems a funny thing now to see all those thousands of houses at Stanmore when I've walked pretty well every inch of it with horses at harvest time. I did it for the money but it was fun too. We used to be able to ride the horses. We'd take them up at nights and wait until they'd had their tea, and then we were allowed to ride them from the stables over to the fields.

Richard Pearce, born 1893

I went to work when I was eleven. Nearly all the boys used to do jobs before they left school, either with paper rounds or cleaning boots and knives in the gentlemen's houses. I worked for George Steel. A most expert confectioner and chocolate maker he was. I got a shilling a day from him and a big bag of cakes to bring home. I just ran the errands. I used to go up Sleepers Hill – walk all the way – and help the bigger boy who was about seventeen push the bread in the truck. Then I went to work for a Doctor Wickham in Jewry Street. I used to go every night and take all the medicines round to the gentry's houses for four and six a week. Then I got another job in a house called Ashdene for a College master by the name of Carter – probably this would have been about 1912 – and I used to clean the boots and knives there. Then whiten the hearth with a hearth brick, and the front step. I used to get eighteen pence a week for that. The thing that stands out in my mind more than anything is the poverty.

Ernest Woolford, born 1904

We lived in Highcliffe, and when I was twelve I used to be at Sharp's bakehouse right up in Station Hill at four o'clock in the morning. The baker would get the dough out of a huge bath and my job was to pull pieces out and roll them in balls of two ounces for doughnuts. Then you flattened one side so that when they were fried, they automatically turned over. I used to work there until eight o'clock. Then I was given a good breakfast and sent to school. After school at four o' clock I used to go up there again until seven o'clock. Saturday I was there all day from eight until six. I would be frying doughnuts and putting jam in the puff pastry triangles. Then I used to put the doughnuts and other cakes in the baker's wheelcart and push them down to Sharp's restaurant in the Broadway. In the afternoon I used to have to scrub the bakehouse out – it was all flagstones – on my hands and knees. While I was doing that the hams were put in the oven by the baker before he went off duty and I had to take them out at three o'clock when they would be cooked. For all that I used to get ten shillings a week. During the winter in very bad weather my mother used to bake potatoes in their jackets and I'd go to work with them in my pocket with my hands wrapped round them. It never done me any harm. Not a bit of harm. I never felt tired. They were furious when I left. I did it for two years until I left school at fourteen.

Herbert North, born 1906

Making yourself useful

At Winnall where it's all built over now, that was all allotments because the working man had to have an allotment to provide for his family. One little job my father used to give me once a week was to go out with a wheelbarrow made out of a Tate sugar box and collect horse manure from the streets. Then it was put on the allotment. We used to get wonderful crops. You could only carry one cauliflower at a time they were so large.

Reginald 'Neill, born c. 1903

My mother took in two people's washing to supplement the family income. On Tuesdays when the ironing was finished everything was carefully folded, with the shining stiff collars on the top, and all was covered with a clean cloth. The people it belonged to lived in two different parts of town and my brother and I had to carry it in a large wicker laundry basket with a handle at each end. It was a bit of a job because one of the places we had to go was at the top of St Giles Hill. There were a lot of steps to climb and it was difficult to keep the basket level. My brother, who was four years younger than me, would sometimes get fed up and drop his end so that I had to carry the lot for the rest of the way. We much preferred the other address, which took us around by Wolvesey where we could collect conkers and beech nuts. Also, the housekeeper gave us both a piece of cake.

Dorothy Yaldren, née Newman, 1903

Saturday morning I'd go to my grandmother's and do the shopping for her, and put an order in for World Stores or the Home and Colonial to deliver. I'd do my mother's shopping too and then lunch time I used to go to the fish and chip shop for several neighbours. After that I would get a wheelbarrow – a sort of box on wheels – and I'd go all the way to Winnall Moors to the gasworks there and get a barrow full of coke for a shilling. Coke was used on the kitchen range because it lasted longer than coal. We didn't use coal to cook by. Cooking on the range was a trial. An effort. Mother would light the fire up and get the oven hot and have the hob with soup going all the time. We were using coke even before wartime coal rationing came in. We were very poor before the war.

Joan Halford, née Edmonds, 1926

We wouldn't have lived very well if my father hadn't produced fresh vegetables all the year round. He had four or five plots. He used to keep chickens and ducks. Some people used to keep pigs on their allotments. After I was about seven or eight, one of my weekly chores was that I went to all the neighbours with a wheelbarrow and collected their swill – potato peelings, cabbage leaves and trimmings from vegetables. I had to push it over the by-pass to my dad's allotment which is terrifying to even think about. He used to boil it all up and mix it with various things to feed the chickens. It used to smell awful, especially in the summer. And this wheel barrow was a wooden thing that he'd fashioned himself – a sort of box on two wheels. It wasn't a lot of fun when I was fourteen and wanted the boys to take an interest in me. I used to try various disguises. Dress as a boy and wear a flat cap and all sorts of things. I was terrified of bumping into somebody I knew.

Annette Hawkins, née Gough, 1949

We boys used to have to help. Every Saturday it was my job to do the dusting. In those days if they had a table it was plastered up with everything. You never saw a bare table top. There was photographs, there was aspidistras, there was ornaments. Every little scrap of wall was filled with photographs or pictures. You could hardly see the wall. And then they'd have a big mirror and this was all ornamented and they would have ornaments stuck on the shelf and that sort of thing. Same with the mantelpiece. That was all tea caddies and things like that. Just imagine taking down and dusting all that. You had coal fires and so plenty of dust did settle. It took me practically all the morning. When I finished one room I'd have to go and do another one and so on.

Jesse Smith, born 1903

There were four of us girls and every Saturday we had our jobs to do. You had to get the knife board out and clean the cutlery because it was silver-plated. Then the brass trays and the brass candlesticks all had to be cleaned. And we had black, white and red tiles running up to the front door and they had to be scrubbed every Saturday.

In those days there was a rag and bone shop in Middle Brook. Dear old Mum, she used to get a rabbit sometimes and she'd skin it and paunch it. Now these rabbit skins weren't thrown away. They were taken up the rag and bone shop. We used to take them up and get a few pence for them. In those days you could get a pound of stewing steak for about sixpence and so that rabbit skin might buy a dinner for the kids. I think the skins were probably sent to make fur gloves and things like that. Even fur coats. Jam jars were another thing we used to have to take up to the rag and bone shop. You'd get a ha'penny for a one pound jar and a penny for a two pound jar.

One day my father had a lot of them so he goes down to Carrie Glover in Chesil Street, and borrows this box on iron wheels from her. He fills it up with jam jars and says to my sister and I, 'Take that up and I'll meet you on the bridge and take the money from

A class at All Saints School, c. 1927. Irene Underwood is the girl in the middle, behind the row of boys at the front.

you.' We didn't like this idea. We were a bit proud and didn't want to push this thing up the High Street. Anyway, he saw us out of the back door and went off but we went straight in again by the front door. We said to Mum we're not going to take this up the High Street and she was lovely she really was. What she did, she unpacked the jars from the barrow and packed them all in a wicker clothes basket and that's how we took the jam jars up to the rag and bone shop.

Irene Underwood, née Clewer, 1916

I remember every so often, Mum making a bundle of rags and woollens and things and my sister and I used to trot down to somewhere in the Brooks where there was a rag and bone shop. The man there used to buy rags and woollens by the pound providing you put cotton in one bundle and woollens in another bundle. We'd come out of there with about three shillings which probably kept my mum going for another couple of days.

Annette Hawkins, née Gough, 1949

One time when I was quite small, and the mayor and corporation and everyone come round to Beat the Bounds, I followed the crowd. This was 1900 and just below the Riflemen's Cottages[23] on the bank they had the ceremony of the stone. They put the stone in the hole and then they called out for a boy. A boy run out and that was me. Picked me up, bashed me on my behind on the stone pretty 'ard and that settled the stone in. I took a dim view of it at the time because I didn't know what was coming off you see. But at any rate they settled me up all right. They gave me half a crown and that was that.

Richard Pearce, born 1893

Sunday

On Sunday from our skin outward we all wore clean clothes, starched knickers (which I hated), and a starched pinny with gophered frills on the shoulders. At ten o'clock we were off to Sunday school in Chesil Street for half an hour, and then across the road to St Peter's church. If there was Holy Communion at the end of the service, we were ushered out by the Sunday School teacher because they said we fidgeted too much. At home, Dad would be waiting to take us to the cathedral to see the soldiers and the band that had been on Church Parade. They marched to the barracks with music playing, and they went on playing on the Barrack Square for half an hour. Then home to mother who had been cooking Sunday dinner – a lovely smell of roast and apple pie. Then to afternoon Sunday School and back home again for tea. On the round wooden bread board, a cottage loaf would be waiting with a pot of jam and sometimes for a treat, a tin of pink salmon or pineapple. Before church again we would stop in the roadway to listen to the Salvation Army band until, at about twenty past six, all the church bells would begin to ring. We would go to the chapel just up the road at the Soldiers' Home as it was called then and their own band would play in the Broadway then from half past seven till eight. Finally we went home to sing round the fire, usually the hymns we had sung that evening, and so, after a drink of cocoa, to bed.

Dorothy Yaldren, née Newman, 1903

The thing I remember most vividly is being taken to the cathedral by my mother, with a white lace dress and blue sash, to what used to be called the Soldiers' Service. They used to march down with a band from the barracks and through the High Street. I think it was probably the Hampshires then and the Rifles. The cathedral nave was absolutely filled with soldiers because attendance was compulsory, but there used to be just a few seats up in the front where the civilians could go. I used to be taken there, largely because it was quite a short service. It lasted about three quarters of an hour and the sermon was never longer than three minutes – so both soldiers and small children were able to bear it you see. Then we used to come out by the Buttercross and watch the soldiers go up the High Street back to the barracks.

I also remember being taken to the cathedral by my father when there was a morning service. I used to get very fidgety, and the cathedral at that time was perfectly filthy. They had enormous stoves about five foot high in which coke was burned and of course they made a tremendous amount of dust and just warmed the small area round about themselves. The rest of the cathedral was like a morgue. I know my father used to be very worried because I always had beautiful white gloves on and used to wipe my fingers along the chairs and this made black marks on them.

Monica Woodhouse, née Stroud, 1911

Monday

Monday was my least favourite day of the week because it was washing day. I got up early as, before school, I had to take a sack and walk for ten minutes to the carpenters and woodcarvers, Thomas's, at the top of Highcliffe Steps. The entrance to the workshop was about half way up the steps. Beside the lathes there were piles of wood shavings on the floor which I and the other kids were allowed to take. They were obviously glad to get rid of them. A big sackful was quite light to carry and when I arrived home, Mother had filled the copper and was ready to stuff the shavings up the 'copper hole' and set fire to them, which soon made the water hot. In the sink was a big bath with the scrubbing board, a smaller one for the 'blue' and another for the starch. The washing would take all day and at dinner time we would only have cold meat from the Sunday joint, bubble and squeak (fried cabbage and potato) and cold apple pie and custard. When I came home from school at half past four, the washing was nearly done and any hot water left was used to scrub the scullery and outside toilet and drain. A handful of soda crystals would be thrown in the bucket and we used a big scrubbing brush, a floor cloth and Sunlight soap. There were sixteen houses in our row [Upper Wolvesey Terrace], with a communal drying ground, a grassy patch behind the houses, with sixteen individual lines. No one dare touch or use any but their own. It was quite a sight on Mondays. On other days it was the kids' playground but on a Monday, if anyone made someone else's washing dirty, there was the devil to pay and sometimes an argument among the mothers as to who did what.

Dorothy Yaldren, née Newman, 1903

Singing in the Choir

We used to play about. Sometimes, the row farthest from the organist thought they were safe but sometimes he'd get fed up. I remember once he got hold of two of them and banged their heads together. You could hear the noise all over the church. He didn't half bang their heads. Other times, the parson might happen to turn round and catch somebody acting the fool. After the service he'd whack the sides of their heads – and he had oh such a big hand. His great big hand right on the ear. Yes, you copped it if you were caught.

Jesse Smith, born 1903

I sang in the choir at Chesil church, where we were always intrigued by one of our bell ringers. He was the captain of the bell ringers – Mr Lampard senior. He used to show off a bit we used to think, because he would ring three bells at once. He had one in each hand and he would ring one with his right foot. His left foot was anchored in a large strap which was firmly fixed to the floor. I suppose to keep him steady while the other limbs were in motion. Chesil Church had a very good choir. Not because I sang in it myself, but they had girls in the choir and they sat in the front row of what you might call the body of the church. About eight of them with their cream capes and white hats. They used to look very pretty too. My mother used to say that their mothers ought to be proud of them the way they turned them out, especially on a Sunday.

Austin Laverty, born 1896

The Central School, c. 1907. Dorothy Nunn's father is third from the right in the front row. Her mother is third from the left in the row behind. Four other family members are also in this class. The girls' loose hair indicates that the photograph was taken on Ascension Day.

Clothing

Looking back, how formal we were in those days, even the children! On no account were we allowed to wear our best Sunday clothes and shoes on a weekday. Whit Sunday especially meant white shoes and stockings for the girls. On Sundays too, if we had long hair, we were allowed to wear it loose, whereas on weekdays it was plaited. Only on one weekday at school could we wear loose tresses with a bow of ribbon and that was on Ascension Day when we went to St Maurice's church in the morning and then had the afternoon off. Of course, there were some children at school who wore boots with their toes poking out and very shabby clothes with torn elbows and frayed sleeves.

Dorothy Yaldren, née Newman, 1903

The kids then were running about with no shoes on their feet and their backsides out of their trousers. But I'll tell you how my mother used to manage. There was a shop on the City Road run by a Mrs Murray. She was one of the first people that let people have their clothes on tick, and mother used to go up there and pay at so much a week.

Ernest Woolford, born 1903

Discipline

If you were a decent family you were brought up strictly. I think the majority of working class families were strict. Some kids used to be hit no end but my parents never used to hit us. My father used to shout at us but he never hit us. My mother didn't even like to hear me say 'silly fool'. She used to say, 'Oh don't talk like that.'

Irene Underwood, née Clewer, 1916

Oh God yes, I was hit as a child. My father used to clout me. We really had to behave ourselves. At meal times we weren't allowed to put our elbows on the table, we weren't allowed to speak and we really had to have perfect manners. Mind you in later life you were grateful for it. It was good training. Do you know, we had a dog and that dog dare not get on the garden. It had to walk round the paths. Father trained it. He was a terror for discipline.

Norman Underwood, born 1915

Mystery

Sexual matters were never talked about – never. You just found out by devious means.

My mother never told me a thing. I remember when it was period time, she asked my aunt to tell me what would happen. As regards sex or anything like that – never ever mentioned. Never. Extraordinary isn't it? I used to wonder, and think now, however did that happen? Where did babies come from? My mother used to say they came from under the gooseberry bush. They were very secretive then. Now they're just the opposite.

Lilian Woolford, née Hibberd, 1907

Horror

Another thing one recollects – I suppose it was because we were living up at Clifton Lodge – was the nearness of the prison. The *awful* thing was the hangings. They hoisted a black flag and I think they tolled a bell but at any rate for children, well one never forgot it. That's why one always thought it was so frightful of Thomas Hardy to have hanged Tess of the D'Urbervilles there.

Amy Stidston née Savage

Excitement

When the barracks burned down in 1894 we saw it all from Highcliffe. We used to go along there and stay for hours watching and it was a brilliant sight. It was smoking for days. The flare from Highcliffe was wonderful.

Arthur W. Hodges, born 1888

If I was asked which day I enjoyed most before the first war, it would be the October fair

The Clewer family, about 1937, outside No. 3 St Catherine's Road. Irene Underwood is third from the left.

which took place at Bar End, about a mile from the city, in the middle of the month. The cattle fair was on the Friday and the fun fair on the Saturday. In those days, cows and sheep were driven along the roads from the outlying farms. There were few motor vehicles, only horse-drawn ones and cycles. The sheep usually straggled right across the road and if some went adrift, we would help round them up for the drover. The animals made an awful mess of the roads but they were cleaned up by the water carts which shot fast jets of water out at the back. Some of the boys would try to ride on the back in the middle of the water. In fact they would try it on any cart that looked easy to hitch a ride on and we 'good' children would shout to the

driver, 'Whip behind Mister!' He would then flick his long whip round the side hoping to frighten the boys off, because he couldn't see them.

On the evening of the fair, when you got to the beginning of Bar End, you could hear the music and the sound of it put wings on your feet and you couldn't get there fast enough. As you got near, there were men selling cheap jewellery, watches and so on by the kerb side. A friend of mine bought a watch for half-a-crown. It looked beautiful as the man showed it round, but when she got it home and opened it to see the 'jewelled works' there were no works, let alone jewels. When you got to the gate there it all was – the helter-skelter, roundabouts, hoopla, the boxing booth, the Fat Lady, the swings and oh, lots more and all lit up – noise, smoke and music. To a schoolgirl it was like walking into Heaven! The boys would chase us and try to put handfuls of confetti down our necks, and just inside the gate was a man making humbugs. He would roll up the sticky mass and pull it until it was about a yard long, then put the ends together and wave it round until it was twisted tightly. Then he slapped it on the table and cut it into humbugs. I liked to watch the shooting booth where there were ducks held up by water jets which were tricky to hit as they bobbed up and down, but my favourite was the helter-skelter on which we whizzed round the tower on a mat.

Dorothy Yaldren, née Newman, 1903

We were always being taken along to see the Diver when he came up. I can remember his helmet being removed. We thought it was so strange. That was quite an entertainment for us.

Beatrice and Mildred Forder

When the circus came they used to let the animals go down and bathe in the River Itchen. At the bottom of Blue Ball Hill there was a kind of a gap in the bank and the animals could step down in. The elephants would get a trunk full of water and you had to look out otherwise you'd get absolutely drenched if they suddenly thought they'd dowse you with a trunk full. But I was never one to give 'em a bun. I was afraid they'd bite me hand off.

Jesse Smith, born 1903

Street Games

People had large families and we were all about the same age, so if so-and-so never turned up there was always somebody else in its place. The games would follow one another at certain times of year. There was marbles, hoops, tops. When it was hoops the girls would have wooden hoops and the boys would have iron ones. We had a kind of a crook with a wooden handle and you'd run along with it so that if you wanted it to stop, you stuck the crook in and pulled the thing back. Sometimes the hoop would run away with you. I remember once it went down the hill and fortunately they had the shutters up or else it would have gone right through the window. Very often, the draymen and other men driving horses would shout at us. They were afraid the hoops would get under the horses' hooves. The tops – one was shaped like a carrot, one like a turnip and another like a mushroom. The mushroom was dangerous because when you whipped it the whip would lift it up and it would go sailing through somebody's glasshouse or something. The carrot and turnip would just spin. Sometimes we made up our own games. Perhaps we'd say that them in the next road along were our enemies, and we'd chase them up and down the street. Get Mother's prop and CHARGE! Course, if Mother's prop got broken you came in for it.

Jesse Smith, born 1903

Cinema

I used to go to St John's Rooms where they had a cinema, in Mr Simpkins day, that was. My father was relief pianist there – in front of the screen – until he got pelted with orange peel and whatnot and they moved the piano behind the screen. We always had a free seat. All the children used to be squashed on the front benches. It was a case of 'move up, move up, move up'. Everybody squashed up until somebody fell off the other end. Father used to improvise the music. He was very good at that. If it was a sad scene he would play 'Hearts and Flowers' or something like that. Even when he was behind the screen he used to do it just the same. He was also relief pianist at another cinema. He used to go off from the umbrella shop for a couple of hours, and then come back looking quite pleased with himself. I suppose that was because of the extra money he used to earn.

Lilian Woolford, née Hibberd, 1907

There was a cinema next door to the *Hampshire Chronicle*. It was a very sordid little place and I remember seeing Rudolf Valentino there several times rather surreptitiously. They had a live orchestra – a piano, violins and I think a cello – playing a lot of wrong notes often, but nobody minded. The cinema was very much frowned on by parents. It was considered a place where you picked up fleas or diseases or coughs and colds and it also prevented you from doing your homework as you should do.

Monica Woodhouse, née Stroud, 1911

Outings and other Pleasures

We always went to the seaside at least once a year. We'd catch a train at about half past seven in the morning and get to Bournemouth about nine. We couldn't get to the sea soon enough and we had a lovely day there. They always chose a nice day, probably in June. We had other kinds of outings too. We used to go nutting. We'd go over Teg Down towards a place called Crab Wood which was full of hazelnut trees. We used to go around September. Make a whole day of it and take a picnic – walk there and back. Yes, we did everything on our feet. I used to like to go picking primroses too, to decorate the church for Easter. We used to go to Littleton for that on Good Friday and nearly always Good Friday was the best day of the four days' holiday. I do remember once we went there and it was intermittent showers, and we saw a lovely rainbow. Beautiful rainbow. Oh yes I used to enjoy me forays into the country. Whenever I was out for a walk in springtime the first dog rose I saw I always put in me buttonhole. A nice little pink bud.

Jesse Smith, born 1903

We used to go to Chilcomb to the country lanes and pick violets on the seventeenth of March. That would be our day out. Going out into the country. It would be lovely going along by the hedges with the wind in our hair in March.

Joan Halford, née Edmonds, 1926

Just before the first war, in about 1912, we went over to Avington Park to pick mushrooms. We were scrumping them really. We used to walk all the way and come home with about fourteen pounds. Once a young keeper ran after me and when he caught me he clipped me under the ear,

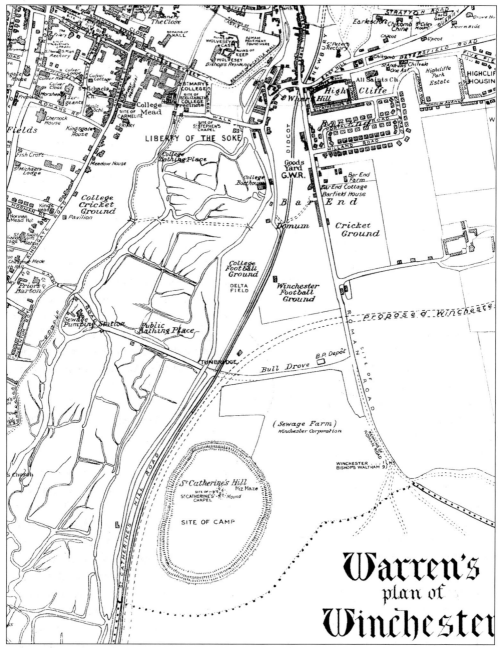

Map of the area to the south-east of Winchester.

emptied my mushrooms on the ground and trod on the lot. We picked another basketful on the way home even though I was crying all the time.

Ernest Woolford, born 1904

When we were children we often went on St Catherine's Hill for picnics. You saw any amount of people then picknicking there. You don't see many people up there now. In those days there was no by-pass and we used to love St Catherine's Hill. One went straight up under the archway near the towpath. Those were the days when there were butterflies – the Chalkhill Blues on that chalk pit. Oh and something wonderful! Beyond Tunbridge, not on the towpath side but on the other side, it led along to a cottage which was owned by Mr and Mrs Bates. Across the canal she had a pulley and a little box, and if you walked along the canal towpath you could ring a bell and Mrs Bates came out and said, 'What do you want?' It was usually a Fry's penny bar of chocolate, but sometimes it was some sort of rather awful cherry cordial and she'd say, 'That comes to twopence. Put your money in the box'. Then she pulled it across and back would come this wonderful concoction. Mrs Bates also did teas. During the summer holidays the townspeople were allowed to use the punts and the boats from the College boathouse and always, on August Bank Holiday, we used to hire two punts and a boat. We would then order tea from Mrs Bates. You either had it in her garden or she handed it out to you and you had it in your punt.

Christmas was wonderful too in those days. We were lucky because we had a musical family. Our father and both our uncles were musical. One uncle was the organist at St Thomas's church and another was at St Maurice's church. We were allowed when we were small children, to go out carol singing and in those days it was a very important event. On the last night we always sang on the Guildhall steps

Amy Stidston, Ruth Stackard (sisters),
née Savage

I remember that our playground was the cathedral yard, because at number twenty-eight The Square, where I grew up, we had no garden. I remember the museum in the Square too. Our father used to take us over there at tea time to see the mangy old lion. We always insisted on going upstairs to see the lion and the crocodile before we were brought in to be put to bed.

Lilian Woolford, née Hibberd, 1907

When I was a boy, Winnall Moors was deliberately flooded for skating. It would be about eighteen inches deep. There were two fields with a hedge dividing them but they made a gap in the middle so that you could go from one lot of ice to another. The very expert skaters wouldn't go through the gap. They would leap over the hedge which was about three feet high and land on the other side. My father used to push me along in a chair while he was skating. All round the outside, the spare room was taken up by people hiring out skates and single chairs for learners. You caught hold of the chair and you pushed the chair while you were learning. Then you had the chestnut vendors all round there and you also had a very long sledge for a big carthorse. He wore leather boots so that he wouldn't spoil the ice. Us children used to go all around the outside on this sleigh and we used to enjoy it, especially with hot chestnuts. They used to have old lamps all around too. It was quite nice to see with all the reflections on the ice, and these lights all the way around. That would go on for anything up to a fortnight every winter. It was frozen hard.

Herbert North, born 1906

On Winnall Moors in summertime, we used to cut a little nick in the bank and let the water come out so that it would flood the lowlands there. And we'd build huts out of branches and have no end of fun down there. We used to pinch potatoes from allotments, light a fire and boil them up and we'd make tea and cocoa in a billy can. Then we'd go in the water and walk up and down in it to make it muddy. We had sticks with brass wire on, made into a slip loop and then when the pike used to poke their heads out of the muddy water we'd slip the wire over them and whssssht! – take them home and eat them.

Ben Kerley, born 1909

We never expected to be taken away. Our parents couldn't afford it. Our holiday was a Sunday School outing to Avington Park, or a day in Lee-on-the-Solent. During the long, hot summers, my friends and I used to get a pennyworth of lemonade powder and make up a bottle of lemonade. We'd make some jam sandwiches and off we'd go up St Giles Hill. We lived so close to it, and it

was lovely. We'd spend the whole day up there and then come home thoroughly tired out. We didn't have any money but they were happy times.

Irene Underwood, née Clewer, 1916

We went for long walks. I used to go with my friends to Farley Mount and back again, walking both ways and thinking nothing of it. On Bank Holidays and times like that one walked to Avington Park and had a picnic or walked to Shawford through the meadows (a most beautiful walk), had a picnic on the downs there, and came back on the train.

Monica Woodhouse, née Stroud, 1911

When we were young in the early twenties, we used to splash out on the occasional dance at the Guildhall. There was a place at the bottom of the High Street – St John's Hall – where they used to have a hop on a Friday night called the 'tanner hop'. We used to go to that. We had some real good fun down there. Everybody went who had sixpence to spend.

Lilian Woolford, née Hibberd, 1907

Swimming

In the park, where the swimming pool used to be, it's all overgrown now. It was just part of the river fenced off and was terribly cold because the water was flowing. It was stony-bottomed and muddy and when the weeds were cut further up the river they would all come through. One of the girls I

Enjoying themselves at the Lido in the 1930s. (HRO 64M86W/23)

was at school with nearly drowned because of this. She'd just learned to swim and was swimming across the deep end with one of the teachers when all this weed came through. She got panicky and caught up in it and went down three times. It wasn't nice to swim there. The other one at Bull's Drove was better, but there again it was only the flowing river fenced off. We used to love going up to the Lido, though. We'd spend our Thursday afternoons there because Thursday was half-day in Winchester. It was open-air and tiled but it was too small for the number of people that got up there. We used to lie in the sun, go for a swim and then try and get off with the boys – the way youngsters do.

Irene Underwood, née Clewer, 1916

The Lido in Worthy Road had a big outdoor swimming pool. You used to go and laze around on the paving slabs, flashing your bikini off and all the rest of it. It was a place where people met and had fun and chatted. In the fifties when you went swimming it was a social occasion. Usually half-a-dozen kids from the street went together. You had your costume rolled up in your towel and if you were lucky, you had a bottle of lemonade. The best thing were the picnics down the meadows near Bull's Drove. If we couldn't afford the sixpence to get into Bull's Drove we used to swim at Tunbridge. It was a nice sunny bank there, and there was room perhaps for half-a-dozen families.

Annette Hawkins, née Gough, 1949

Self-improvement

When I was small, my mother would sometimes take me to the cathedral and I remember the effect the singing and the wonderful organ-playing had on me. Naturally, I had no opportunity to study music. Then at seventeen a little madrigal group needed a bass and I was dragged into it. The girl who played the piano taught me the bass parts and I gradually began to enjoy the singing. Soon afterwards I joined Holy Trinity church choir and became friendly with Patrick Mace, the youngest son of the Reverend Mace. I think it was probably that which made me feel I had to do something about educating myself. When I began singing in the choir I couldn't read music which I found very frustrating, so I bought an old crock of a piano and settled down to teach myself to play and to unravel the mysteries of musical notation. When I was twenty-one I had my first piano lessons. I was then singing in the Hyde Festival Choir and Miss Lilian Brown who was the conductor offered to take me on as a pupil at half fees. I suspect she felt sorry for me. She taught me piano technique. When I was twenty-four, there began a two-year German course on the radio which I followed right through. I just studied and studied everything really.

William Blackman, born 1908

CHAPTER 6
Employment, Work and Business

A Struggle to survive

People just used to do their work. Most men never left off work until about six o'clock at night, and by the time they got home they were tired. They were glad to go to bed because they had to be up at six to start at seven o'clock. Some men started before that. They used to work, and didn't get hardly any wages. It was a constant worry from morning to night, day in and day out, the way to live and how to feed and clothe the children. We know things were cheaper – but you had to get it first. In the days when an ordinary man earned fifteen shillings a week my dad was a tip-top gardener. He was experienced inside and out. He ran a garden and the most he ever earned in all his life was a pound a week. People now have got the money and they've got the pleasures. In the old days they had no money and they had no pleasures – only what they made themselves, and that was precious little. Things these days [1969] are heaps better. I wouldn't like to see the old days back again.

Richard Pearce, born 1893

Everybody had large families – ten children often. Everybody had to work. No dole.

You had to work or starve. It was just hand-to-mouth. People in those days never had holidays. Or only one day. Men on firms had one day a year. They used to have horse brakes to drive them to London or the seaside or wherever they wanted to go. But they only had one day, and they used to have to pay in so much for that.

Gertrude Asher, née Whittier, 1880

In those days before the First World War, I guarantee that if you put up in your window 'Man Wanted,' before that had been up a half-hour there would have been a dozen men in for that job. You see there was no industry at all. It was only agricultural labourers or such like who were wanted. There was a bit of building and painting and that. The thing was, if you had a job you had to stick it. I delivered coal. I worked seventy-four hours a week. We never got paid until we had finished on a Saturday night. A married man had to go home with his money about nine o'clock at night and the wife had to come up to town shopping. Underwoods – that was a big grocer – they was open 'til eleven and twelve on a Saturday night.

Arthur W. Hodges, born 1888

Alderman Forder's Wool Business in Lower Brook Street

The warehouse was the biggest in the south of England for wool, and was built by father's grandfather. It was very strongly built and had wonderful iron posts. Father used to tap on the iron post – with one of these great hooks that you put into sacks – for the foreman to come down, and the foreman would slide down one of the spiral slides. They weren't really spiral though. We used to call them slopes. You went down this one from one floor to the next. Then just round the corner and down the next one. They were made of wood. Mr

W.H. Forder in 1899, father of Beatrice and Mildred Forder. (HRO 2M88W/19)

Baker used to roar down it! When we were children it was our greatest delight to get one of the sacks and go down the slide.

Father used to go all over the place, to farms in Dorset and all around to buy wool on the sheep's back as it were. It would come in from the farms and from the Isle of Wight and so on, and they would catch it with a couple of great iron hooks. It came in as raw wool and went out in bales sorted for a particular purpose to go to various other manufacturers. The best would go to Paton's for making their yarn. The wool was sorted in the warehouse and we used to watch the sorters standing at a table which was like a wire tray very similar I think to the kind of tray on which paper is made. The wires only went in one direction, and it was there to enable any dirt and grit to drop through. It wasn't washed then you see. There are fourteen sorts of wool on a sheep's back and the speed with which they took up a ball of sheared wool and sorted it out! The wool used to be made up into the most enormous bales, the width of this room.

They were all craftsmen who worked there. There was a Mr Hayter, who came there at fourteen and remained there until he died over seventy. The men used to live around there in the Brooks and spent their whole lives in it. They had stopped making parchment in father's day, but he used to have pelts brought and they were dressed in the lime pits because the river ran just there you see. There was a series of lime pits. As children of course we were always kept strictly away from them. There were about ten of these great square pits and white all over. The men used to draw the pelts out with enormous, long tongs. I remember seeing the man who stripped the skin. He placed it over an enormous

Forder's wool store in Lower Brook, 1916. (HRO 2M88W/22e)

horseshoe-shaped piece of wood. It had a curved blade. A very sharp, two-handled blade and he was so skilled that he stripped the skin until it was I think seven layers. Seven layers to a sheep's skin and it's the one nearest the tissues that makes the parchment. The outer one is the hide. I don't know what they used the other layers for. I wonder if there is any craftsman in the country who can do that now [1979]. Dollery used to strip the skins; he lived in

St John's Street. Matthews lived in St John's Street as well. Many of the cottages in Poulsom Place, which used to run at right angles to Lower Brook Street and ran to the back of the bus station, were built by our great-grandfather for his employees. They've all been pulled down now [1979]. We were great pals with the men. We used to try and get in there when father wasn't looking. When our grandfather was alive he was frightfully severe on us and we had to keep ourselves well out of the way. We used to peep through the keyhole to see if he was in the office. We daren't go in if he was.

Beatrice and Mildred Forder

Andrews' Eating House

My grandfather Andrews had an eating house in Cross Keys Passage. Grandpa Grey had it before him. They had faggots, peas, chips, gravy, boiled pork belly and all sorts of pies. The smell was absolutely out of this world. Everybody knew Andrews'. The Americans who came over in the First World War used to speak of Bill Andrews' faggots, peas and chips, and so of course when the Americans came back during the Second World War, they used to want to go and sample what their fathers had sampled. They sat down at a scrubbed table which, I hasten to add, I used to have to help scrub from time to time. The room had a kitchen stove in it and was exactly the same as it had been when my mum was a little girl. And regularly, every Saturday, the gypsies came in from the country – the Castles, the Barneys, the Wilsons. They were the loveliest and kindest people out, they really were. Yes, Grandpa Grey started the eating house and Uncle Fred finished it about 1954. The recipe for the faggots died with him.

Dorothy Nunn, née Bath, 1927

People loved them, people talked about them, people still talk about them – those wonderful, famous faggots. It couldn't have been expensive there because my mother could afford it. She took me in a few times. It was magic behind that door in Cross Keys Passage.

Annette Hawkins, née Gough, 1949

The gipsies all used to come into town on Saturdays and they all went into Andrews to have their faggots, chips and peas. They parked all their horses and carts in the yard of the Coach and Horses, which was about where the back of Sainsbury's is now. Then in the afternoon they'd have racing up and down Silver Hill. They used run with the horses and people used to bet on them. Then they'd have a few fights and go back off out into the country again.

Louisa Lewis, née Salter, 1918

Wartime Opportunities for Women

I left school at thirteen and a half during the First World War, after I had seen an advert in the paper for a junior to learn the printing trade. As there was a shortage of men at that time females came into their own and I got the job and started as a compositor to a jobbing printer – Mr Taplin in St Swithun Street. I used to do the magazines for different places. There was Durley I always remember. That parson always wrote such a long piece for his magazine and he was such a terrible writer that by the time I'd set this type up you couldn't read it. It was like double Dutch. It was put on the galley and then a sheet was pulled up and you had to read it to see where the mistakes were. I was only a kid and I put down what I thought his letters were supposed to say. When it was

Printers at work in Warren and Sons, about 1915, not long before Dorothy Yaldren was employed there.

drawn up some of it was terribly funny because it didn't make any sense at all. Then Mr Taplin took over and took out all the wrong letters and made sense of it, and then it would all be put together in what they call a 'chase'. It was fitted into the machine and in that particular place it was done with a foot machine – a treadle. There was no motor or anything like that. I learned the basics of printing and, of course, what went on in the different villages. You got used to their writing after a while and where I'd made mistakes in the beginning I got to know better. But my ambition was to get to Warren and Sons for they really were the people. I went to Warren's – I think I was about fifteen – and I worked on what they call the 'platen' machine which was the same as the one at Taplin's but of course they had a big engine room. I was there when the war finished and everybody went mad, and they turned off the engine outside and we packed up work and went out in the High Street and everybody was going crazy cheering.

Dorothy Yaldren, née Newman, 1903

The Craftsman

Most craftsmen used to start at six or seven in the morning. They would work until eight and then they would have breakfast and start again at a quarter to nine. They would go on until twelve o'clock, then start again at one and work till six. No tea break but they didn't seem too bothered. Then if

George and Hannah Bath (seated centre) with their family in the garden at St John's South, c. 1933. Their son Fred who married Rosa Andrews is standing on the left with his wife. Their daughter Dorothy is at the left, in the front row. George Bath was Porter of St John's for thirty-eight years.

they were doing overtime, they went on from a quarter to seven to a quarter to nine. An artisan of that time was doing himself pretty well if he was getting thirty shillings a week. It was sixpence an hour. The young men I knew were very thrifty and they could get first class digs. Board and lodging for seven and sixpence a week. Then, if they were fond of the glass, they could go and have six pints a night for six days a week for

six bob. Twopence a pint. So seven and six and six bob, and cigarettes were very reasonable and he was always well-dressed. He would never wear a coat or a suit on a Sunday that he had worn on a weekday. Once he'd worn that suit on a weekday he'd get another one for Sundays. Still had five shillings he could put in the Post Office, which he always did.

There was definitely more thrift about

then. Where I was up to the first war, money was never mentioned. They weren't worried about how much money they were getting or their colleagues were getting. I happened to be working on a grammar school for a time, and their salary sheet used to come along on a piece of foolscap with the headmaster's name on the top and the second master, and then they'd go down the list according to their seniority and with all the money there and they used to be paid and sign for it. No-one at the bottom ever bothered about what the man at the top was getting. They knew that he'd got to the top and one day if all was well they would be in that position. Salaries were never mentioned. When the second war came along, that all changed.

Austin Laverty, born 1896

The Porter of St John's and his Family

My grandfather was Porter of St John's from 1894 until he retired in 1932 and went to live in number seventeen St John's North. My grandmother had to look after the domestic side of things and be a carer come jack-of-all-trades as well as looking after her family. My Dad, Uncle Jack, Auntie Kit and Auntie Bessie were all born in St John's South where the family had accommodation. Matron would tell granny if anyone was poorly, and ask her to attend them. Granny would make sure they had a clean bed and she would take round a jug of hot vegetable soup that she'd made. In winter if a lot of them were ill it was hard work for her. Grandfather had to look after all the premises and gardens both North and South. He was in charge of the upkeep

generally and he had to make sure that the committee room was absolutely tip-top. It was a lovely room with a long, dark wooden table in it. To me it was a palace. It had a big fireplace which I used to love cleaning. When I went to stay with my grandparents as a small child I would say to granny, 'Please let me clean the grate'. I always liked cleaning. I used to get filthy because it was black-leaded. I used an emery paper thing on it too which we got from Kingdons.

Dorothy Nunn, née Bath, 1927

The Tailor

I worked from eight in the morning until eight in the evening when the curfew rang. I reckon, if I could have had one of these hearing aids years ago I could have held down a better job. I never really liked tailoring but I thought, well, that's it. I went into tailoring and stayed there all my life. When I was thirteen I was apprenticed with a Mr Clifton. You were apprenticed for five years and you sat cross-legged. That wanted some doing. I had ever such a job to sit cross-legged. We sat on benches like boards and the only time we could get off the board was when we did pressing. Sometimes we did pressing by having a board across our legs. The irons were heated in a coke oven and you fished them out with an iron crook because the handles would be as hot as the irons themselves. If you left them too long you had to cool them by dipping them in a bucket of water. There were quite thirty men there on the two floors.

We were paid piece work. It would be a certain amount of money for making a coat but there would probably be extras. If it was a double-breasted coat, that would be a bit extra. Or if it had slits at the side or a slit at the back that would be a bit extra. If you made [evening] dress and it had silk reveres and that, that would be a penny an hour extra. That was supposed to be high class work.

We could come in when we liked but we only got paid for what we did. In summer, when you could work all the hours of the day and night, you had to put money aside for the slack times that came after Christmas. In the summer when you'd like to have a break you couldn't afford to. Being situated here with all the country around, Clifton's did very well. We had quite a reputation with the gentry – Lord and Lady This and Sir Somebody Else That. I don't know whether there is anyone in the town can do tailoring now [1987]. I was one of the younger ones in the trade because nobody was going into it any more.

Jesse Smith, born 1903

The Apprentice Dressmaker

In 1921 when I was fourteen I was apprenticed to Madam Rita. At that time she was at the top of the Square facing down it. She had workrooms right at the very top, and the little shop where she used to fit and interview clients was down on the street. She had some very good clientele. County people used to come in there. When I first went I used to have long walks to Park Road and various places round the city delivering the dresses. I used to have to say, 'Please can I have the box back?' In a big house that's been pulled down now in Park Road, a lady's maid used

to come to the door – very, very smart with a bright red dress and a frilly apron. I didn't mind delivering because I got out in the fresh air. I worked nine o' clock until five. Wasn't much money though. Five shillings and sixpence I think I had to start. Mother had the five shillings and I had the sixpence pocket money. I was there just on four years until I was married. You didn't really qualify. Your money just went up year by year. From five shillings perhaps you went to nine and then maybe fifteen.

Lilian Woolford, née Hibberd, 1907

The Housewife

Before the Second World War, it was the man who brought the money home. A married woman wouldn't dream of going to work. No matter how poor one was, the wife didn't go out to work at all. She had to work in the home and bring the family up, knit and sew, make the children's clothes and be the proper housewife. It was hard work, especially when there was a large family and everything had to be done in the scullery. In my grandmother's house there was just a horrible stone sink in there. No draining board or anything. She had a big table beside the sink that she had to do everything on and behind her, when she was stood at the sink, was the great big copper. If she needed any hot water for washing or baths or anything like that she would have to carry buckets of water from the sink to the copper and fill it up and then light a fire underneath. The white stuff was always boiled – sheets and pillowcases and things like that. Then they were rinsed several times and in the final rinsing water she would insert a blue bag to

Nos 5-10 Canon Street in 1956. (HRO W/C5/10/23)

get the water blue. She would put her hand in to see how deep the blue was before the final rinse that would make your washing look snow white. They always did that before they hung it out on the line. It was just hard luck if the wind blew too hard and your line broke, because in those days when they swept the chimneys the soot was thrown over the garden. So then you would have to boil everything all over again because soot is so greasy.

Women never went out to work because they had too much to do in the house. It was hard on the women. There weren't such things as gas fires or electric fires or anything like that. They had to get up early in the morning, they'd have to chop the wood, get the paper ready, start to clean fireplaces out and lay the fires ready for when they were to be lit in each room. There was always the kitchen range to be cleaned out. Not only cleaned out but polished with some sort of blacking. The fireplaces were always beautifully clean and highly polished in spite of them being coal fires.

Joan Halford, née Edmonds, 1926

Laundry Work

Nearly all of the women in Middle Brook worked in the Snow White Laundry. A Mrs Hood was the owner of that. It was in Chesil Street, up around by the station. It wasn't such hard work as it had been once because it had machinery. Anything flat used to go through the calenders and then they'd fold it. The smell of the laundry used to be lovely. There was a steam laundry too in Gordon Road which is still there now.

Louisa Lewis, née Salter, 1918

Errand Boy at the India Arms

The day after I left school, I heard that there was an errand boy's job going at the India Arms and I went there, and he took me on. It was from seven in the morning till one in the afternoon. He did a fried fish thing from the back of the yard and I used to go round all the pubs with this cold fried fish, which they then sold. He paid me the normal errand boy's wage, which was eight shillings a week, but most of the errand boys had to work perhaps 'til six o' clock in the evening, so he was a very kindly man. I always remember him with a great deal of affection because he treated me like a father that really I never had, and if he found that anywhere in the afternoon someone wanted some jobs done or other, he'd put me on to them. Once, somebody else told me about a job in St Swithun Street where they wanted someone to clean the shoes and the knives with the old-fashioned machine. I mentioned it to my boss and he said I could go up to the station and push the fish down in a wheelbarrow and then go round and do the job and then come back and go on working. I did that for many years. So I probably got a few more bob a week for that. I don't remember how much now, but one way and another I reckoned I was getting on for some sort of millionaire!

William Blackman, born 1908

Shop Work

I stayed at Warren's until I had an accident on my bike which nearly cut my little fingers off. In the end Mr Warren wrote to my parents and said how sorry he was, but I would have to go because the machine was idle. I was heartbroken. Anyway the manager at Warren's, his wife had the Health Shop along Southgate Street, next to Bright's the paper shop. They lived over the shop and his wife wanted me to go and help her. She liked to have a lie down in the afternoon and I could then take over. Yes, I enjoyed that. For one thing you knew the prices of everything. I can remember Ovaltine for instance. It was one and six, two and six and four and six. But the thing was then, especially if someone had a biggish order, you had to be adding up as you were taking the things down from the shelf. And then you had to take the brown paper which was under the counter and make a parcel and string it all up. Today, they don't have to think even. I stayed for three years.

Dorothy Yaldren, née Newman, 1903

I was fourteen when I left school and started work for Prangnell's the bakers. I worked there for two years serving in the shop from Monday to Saturday. On Saturday we didn't finish until the last loaf of bread was sold. If that was nine o'clock then it was nine o'clock. Then there was all the glass to be cleaned, and the counters and everything had to be spotless. I started off with eight shillings a week doing a forty-eight hour week. Six shillings of that went to my mother so on

Baker to Winchester College.

Established 1855.

S. PRANGNELL,

Baker, Confectioner, *and* Pastrycook,

3, EASTGATE STREET, WINCHESTER.

Deliveries to all parts of the City Daily.

"HOVIS," "CARR'S MALT," AND "WHOLEMEAL" BREAD.

ALL KINDS OF CAKES & CONFECTIONERY MADE TO ORDER.

WEDDING, BIRTHDAY, & CHRISTENING CAKES A SPECIALITY.

NOTED HOUSE FOR "HOME-MADE" CAKES.

Warren's Winchester Directory, 1906.

Sunday morning I would go in early and, on my hands and knees, I would scrub the shop floor. After lunch I would go back and prepare sandwiches and cakes ready for opening the little restaurant there in the afternoon. Numerous people used to come into the tearoom, especially cyclists. They used to leave their cycles by King Alfred's statue. That's how I earned money to buy clothes. Mostly I had hand-me-downs from my aunts.

When I left Prangnell's I went to D.C. Edmonds as a cashier. The buyers for the various departments lived in and they were very hoity-toity. They spoke down to you. Some of the girls who worked on the counters also lived in and they thought that because they were shop assistants they were a little above the class. I didn't like that at all. I only stood

it for nine months and then I went to Lipton's. I liked being behind the counter again but it was a dreadful place to work because of the manager. He didn't trust anyone in the shop so he put his wife in there as an assistant. He used to cheat the customers too, and they were my neighbours so I only stayed six months. Then I went into Woolworths's where I was very happy on the toiletry counter.

We had a tea bar in those days in Woolworth's and we had all the soldiers and that coming in for their cups of tea and sticky buns in their time off. We saw lots of people and had lots of fun. I was a Woolworth girl and proud of it. We had to be educated. We had to be courteous. We had to be smartly dressed. The uniform was rust-coloured. Like an ordinary dress and not like an overall. It

Louisa and Ernest Lewis in the 1950s.

went well with the lovely polished counters that we had. I'd like to see the old store back again. Miss Clinton was manageress there for many, many years.

Joan Halford, née Edmonds, 1926

When my husband had worked his way up to become manager of Macfisheries I went in and worked with him. One thing we did was to put herrings onto these iron rods and take them around to a smokehouse they had in Silver Hill next to a little chapel there. We used to go round to the sawmill in Gordon Road and collect sawdust which we put in a sort of pit underneath the herrings. Then it was set alight and used to smoulder all night. In the morning they were bloaters. All

warm. Lovely! And we'd take them round the shop.

Louisa Lewis, née Salter, 1918

The Hampshire Chronicle

My father was a reporter on the *Hampshire Chronicle* staff and one of my earliest recollections is going in a horse-drawn brake with him to a flower show at Worthy Park. The smell of trodden grass will always bring back those days to me because I was very fond of flower shows. Father would have a basket balanced on his lap containing two pigeons, so that when he had made a note of the winners of the various classes he would write it out, roll it into a container, attach it to the pigeon's leg and then release the pigeon who would fly back to Winchester so that the results would go in that week's paper. Outside his office window there was a flat board like a shelf where the pigeons landed. The Linotype operators would be on the look out for them. Probably the war put an end to that, or else they had a telephone installed. The *Hampshire Chronicle* came out on a Saturday night then and my father's last job was to see it onto the midnight train.

Jessie Canfield, née Dixon, 1903

I think we only had two senior reporters. I remember Tom Dixon as an absolutely first class one. The other one was quite old and rather cantankerous, but his speciality was the agricultural shows and all the agricultural things. He knew all the farmers and he used to take himself off, say for three days, to the Bath and

West. Nothing would be seen of him and then he'd come back with about six columns of copy, all of which had to be printed. Not a word erased. His writing was perfect. Absolute copybook. The standard of writing was extremely good in those days. Looking back perhaps their style was a little flowery but the English certainly flowed. They knew how to write and the meaning was always clear. Funerals were reported with the names of all those present except the ones who inadvertently got left out. My father used to be rather cynical about it. He said that a lot of people used to go to funerals just to get their names in the paper. Before the war, when one knew everybody, one went down the back streets to avoid them in case they stopped one and said, 'Why wasn't my name in so-and-so's funeral report?' That was a hardy perennial. When it came to a big wedding in a 'county' family there used to be a house party for three or four days and I remember very well one of our ancient reporters was always invited to spend time in the house. Then you'd have about three columns about the wedding. Everybody who was there and a full list of the wedding presents down to the mustard spoon. There were no typewriters until I brought a portable home in 1936. My father said, 'We don't want that contraption here!' but before long he was wanting me to type all his letters.

Monica Woodhouse, née Stroud, 1911

The Turf Accountant

My father always had an eye to the main chance and he started this bookmaker's business in about 1910. It was very selective and they used to have to be in Debrett or something to get on his books. He wouldn't take just anyone. It was just a business operation, and he couldn't even tell you where the racing was until he got to his office and looked in the paper. I don't know whether I should say this but among his clients were a number of church dignitaries. You see they could only do it on the sly couldn't they? They couldn't very well ask the gardener to put two bob each way on for them. Not that he would have taken two shillings. As I say, you had to be fairly well off. I don't know how they collected their winnings. Oh and of course the College masters were very keen on it too.

William H.C. Blake, born 1905

Long Hours, low Pay and the Difficulties of obtaining Employment

When I started my business in 1935 I put an advertisement in the paper because I wanted men to carry out the treatment of the deathwatch beetle at Winchester Cathedral. I offered them two pounds and fifteen shillings a week. That was five bob above the normal building rate. And with no time off for weather. I put that in the advertisement you see because a builder would get nothing if it was pouring with rain and he was on an outside job. Do you know, I had a queue of men along the Andover Road waiting to see me about that job? I only wanted three men and about thirty turned up

Stanley Richardson, born 1906

A store in Bar End Road used by Ernest Woolford and his father for their building business, 1950s. Highcliffe steps lie beside it, next to Highcliffe Works. (HCLS)

When we first came to Winchester in 1934 we had a staff at the Stanmore Hotel of about eight. The chef was paid two pounds a week. He used to live out but he had his beer. He had a pint of beer at lunch time and he had a pint of beer in the evening. When we first came he had one half day off a week. He worked every Saturday and Sunday. Betty the maid had thirteen and six. She had all her keep and with her tips she used to manage to put money into the savings bank. We used to charge three and a half guineas for full board for a week.

Cyril and Muriel Taylor

When I left school at fifteen I tried to get into the General Post Office in Winchester. I went for an interview and was accepted but just as I was leaving, this man asked me to sign a form. When I went to do so with my left hand he said, 'I'm terribly sorry. We can't employ you because you're left-handed.' I went home and cried my eyes out. I thought I was a freak.

Rhoda Biles, née Knight, 1921

When I came back to Winchester in the late 1930s, I was out of work for a month. Quite honestly it was the only time in my life I was ever out of work and to me it was a devastating experience. I've always felt sorry to this day for anyone that's unemployed. I found it extremely difficult to get a job. I don't know why but I fancy there must have been a certain amount of unemployment in Winchester then. Eventually I went to Hilliers for a couple of years until the war, although in those days Hilliers had an extremely bad reputation for conditions and especially pay. The agricultural rate that most of the chaps on the ground there were getting was thirty-two and six a week. I don't know what that would be today but it was a very low wage to keep a family on and there wouldn't have been any Social Security or Child Benefit or anything like that. It was very low, but by virtue of my [previous] head-gardenership, I started at two pounds a week with a promise of more if I suited them. After about three months I reminded them of that and got a five bob rise and a few months after that, I got another half-crown rise without even asking for it. After that I think I was the most detested bloke on Hilliers. But I was working away most of the time because they sent me to take charge of gardens where the head gardener was ill or had left suddenly, or to do a day's planting. I was there two years until the Second World War broke out. Hilliers was a luxury trade and they really panicked and got rid of nearly three quarters of their staff almost at once. But to be fair to them they had lots of contacts and they found all of us jobs.

William Blackman, born 1908

Killing Work

I joined the gas works in 1945 and had about five years as a stoker with these big boilers for making steam. Then I had a year or two on the building before I went back scavenge burning at the pumping station down Garnier Road. 'Scavenge' was all the rubbish. We used to burn nearly all of it there you know. They've done away with all the pumps and the chimney now. After nearly a hundred years I suppose. The College kicked up because when they played cricket they used to get the smoke come down sometimes. Well we used to burn the stuff and get rid of near enough all of it. What we didn't they could bury.

On top of that we used to do all the pumping of the sewerage. All that was pumped up by steam. Mind you it was a killing job. We had three shifts. They consisted of four men on the boilers and the engine room, and then another couple of men in the yard for cleaning up

Victor Gough, father of Annette Hawkins. (PG)

103

and manning the tractor that pushed the stuff over towards you, so you could feed it in the furnaces through a manhole. We used to have to stand above the furnaces to do this. And those plates used to be so hot that well, I'll tell you honestly that if we see any boots come down there, even odd ones, and they were better than what we had on (because the heat burnt the soles of your boots off) then we used to put them on the side and chuck ours in and put the other pair on. That'll tell you how hot it was. And at the back, where all the heat went to go round and make the steam, you could put a half-grown colt in there (a dead one chucked in to destroy it) and in less than half an hour there would hardly be any of its shoes left. It was burnt right up. And that was at the back, not on the fire. Terrific heat we used to get out of that. That was from burning all the rubbish. Clinker and bottles and old tin cans all burnt up. We used to fill a furnace up then take our shirts off, wring them out and put them on the boiler to dry. Then we'd pick up another shirt that had been dried in the same way, shake it out and put that one on. That'll show you what hard work it was. It was so hot there that we wanted the corporation to put fans in but they wouldn't do it. Then one day I was talking to this chap about having a strike because of trying to get the fans. That was at two o'clock. I went home and at half past two he was dead. Another one dead from the job. That's when I decided it was time to pack it in. I'll tell you it wasn't many minutes after he died before they had some sort of fans in there to let the air through. I'd fought them for two years to get proper showers put in so we could go under them. The day I left they started putting them in. If you knew your job there it wasn't all that hard but it was the heat.

Victor Gough, born 1908

CHAPTER 7
The Second World War

The Outbreak of War

The outbreak of war that Sunday morning I can remember so well. Everyone was so stunned and I remember Brian, my son, had gone up the road to get the paper. My husband rushed up the road and dragged him back home. You see we didn't know what was going to happen. My husband said that he would have to get to the camp and said that the best thing we could do, instead of going down our air-raid shelter on our own, was to go in next door with the people there. He went off in the car and I went next door where a couple with two children lived – but they weren't there. So, I went to the next house along. My next door neighbour was in there with her children and there was a young couple with a new baby. The mother was crying and the man of the house had his mother in bed in the sitting room. We all went in and sat around and nobody said anything much. We were all shaking with fright with our gas masks ready in case anything happened. Nothing happened for a while and then the man of the house said, 'Can you smell gas?' and somebody else said, 'Yes I can smell gas!' And then we all said yes we could smell gas.

So what could we do? We all put our gas masks on. Anyway after a bit he went out to have a look around. What he'd done was to put the meat in the oven and forgotten to light the gas![24]

Dorothy Yaldren, née Newman, 1903

British Troops

We had so many regiments here. We had the Black Watch at Bushfield. I used to go down there to the dances and one night we had a lot of Scottish dancing. I'd done Scottish dancing at school and I won a prize for it that evening. It was a Boots voucher. The Black Watch had their lovely kilts on and their trews – it was so colourful. My grandmother used to have one of the Scottish soldiers staying with her because his home was too far away to get back there on leave very often. His name was George Fraser and his father was a butcher. When he did get home he used to bring back joints and haggis in his suitcase for my mother and grandmother. He was always so friendly and he used to do a lot with the children. One of the things he did was to go to the Saturday morning pictures and swing the clubs for them. A lot of the servicemen would do things like that. There were an awful lot of good lads in those days.

We also had the Irish Fusiliers with their mustard-coloured kilts and their green tops. They used to dance on Sunday afternoons in the park and give displays of Irish dancing and the pipes. And we had the Royal Corps of Signals here in the Broadway and the Bomb Disposal up at the Lido in Worthy Road. We had the Royal Fusiliers too, and the Warwickshire Regiment. They were all Brummagem boys and full of fun and life. There wasn't enough doing for them in Winchester so sometimes they made their own fun and got into trouble. When the war started

Monica Woodhouse who became Editor of The Hampshire Chronicle in 1939. After the death of her father Arthur Stroud in 1950, she and her husband became joint proprietors. (HC)

RAF Worthy Down was taken over by the Fleet Air Arm so we had them too.

Then there were the Airborne here at Barton Stacey. The Red Berets we called them. When I was in Woolworth's on the toiletry counter, so many of them on a Saturday afternoon would come in and say, 'Joan, any razor blades? What toothpaste have you got? Got any nice soap?' They used to like Lux if you could get it. They were very fond of their soaps, the soldiers. I remember one of them, a Lancashire boy only about nineteen called Johnny Greenall. He only ever bought Gibbs Dentrifice, the solid pink block, and he had the most beautiful teeth. I went to the pictures with him once or twice. Just as a friend, you know. Then years later when I went to Arnheim to see the war graves, he was there with his mates and all the boys from Barton Stacey that I knew. I looked on the roll of memorial and saw all their names.

Joan Halford, née Edmonds, 1926

Canadian Troops

The Canadians were a lot of laughs. They used to come into the YMCA, and one night my cousin and I were dancing with them. All of a sudden I looked down and saw that they had their trousers rolled up, showing off Scotch plaid socks. They all had different colours. It just seemed hilarious when everybody else was in khaki with creases down their trousers. These Canadians didn't give a darn about anything. They were all from farming country in Saskatchewan and places like that. I was very friendly with one of them because his aunt lived just a few doors away from me. Her brother had emigrated to Canada and his son Norris happened to be stationed in Winchester. So of course he made his home with his aunt and his cousins. Sometimes when he was fed up and didn't know what to do, I would take him for bike rides around the city and show him places of interest. Norris came through the war, but so many of the Canadians were killed. They were a smashing crowd.

Joan Halford, née Edmonds, 1926

American Troops

I felt that we were completely swamped by Americans during World War Two but Winchester seemed to flow on underneath somehow. I remember getting into frightful hot water with some American officer who summoned me to his presence because I had published a letter in the *Hampshire Chronicle* from a black American who resented a club in St Thomas's Street being taken over by the whites. It was just quite a mild little letter which said why should they have it? I thought I was going to be court-martialed. I told him, 'You don't know what the freedom of the press is in this country. You'll have to learn.' But of course one did have to be very careful what one published – all the business of the build-up for D-Day and so forth. An interesting time one way or another.

Monica Woodhouse, née Stroud, 1911

No. 4 Black Swan Buildings. The Bureau was set up by the Winchester branch of the English Speaking Union. One of its functions was to arrange visits by Americans to English homes in the area.(HRO 65M90W/88)

We had so many Americans here during the war. They literally took the whole of the city over. I don't recall seeing many negroes though. There were lots of Military Police patrolling all the streets in their steel helmets. They really kept strict order. I remember vividly meeting the Americans. There was one time when I hadn't been out for five months because I'd had a boyfriend who'd been killed. But I did love dancing, and one evening a friend of mine came and said there was a dance at the Guildhall. Well, you never missed an opportunity of going to the Guildhall, especially with the orchestras that they used to have there. The Big Band Sound you would call it now. So I went but I didn't bother to dress up because I didn't feel like dancing. When we arrived there wasn't an English soldier to be seen. Not a sailor either, and we had lots of sailors at Worthy Down. It was all Americans and I thought 'Oh dear!' and went and sat up in the balcony. I watched these Americans below and after a while I thought, 'Poof! I thought Americans could dance. They can't dance for toffees!' I was only, what, seventeen. Then during the interval I went downstairs and one of them pulled me onto the dance floor and wouldn't take no for an answer. So I thought 'Well I've been watching you and you're not a bad dancer. Right! I'll let you have it.' So I started and just went to town and thought I'll show them how English girls can dance. And I did!

Another time I was invited with Woolworth staff to go to an American dance over at Stockbridge camp. We were taken over there by bus and had to go straight in at the door. We weren't allowed to move outside the hut at all. There was a guard each side to make sure that we didn't go anywhere that we shouldn't do. Well it turned out to be an American Airforce band and when they played *In the Mood*, I realised I was actually dancing to Glen Miller because no one could play *In the Mood* the way he could. Especially when it gets to the part where it stops, pauses and then goes on again. The roar of the crowd as he started playing again! The troops went mad over that. It was tremendous. A really fantastic evening.

Of course we were rationed during the war so we used to like to go to dances like these because of the refreshments. I remember one I went to, where there was this huge great big load of cheese on the table and people were just breaking it off by the handful. I had more cheese in my hand than was a month's ration. I really made a pig of myself. If the girls wanted to go to American dances they had to be registered as hostesses. They had to have a card which enabled them to go in, because they had to be screened you see. The Americans were very particular about the type of girls they allowed into their dance halls. You weren't allowed outside with the Americans or anything like that. It wasn't allowed for them to take you home. You would have to get back on to the coach and the coach would take you home. There were one or two Americans who went out with the girls, but not many Winchester girls married Americans. Most of those that did came back again. Not many stayed out there. None of them liked it out in America. It was a different life altogether.

They did like to eat, the Americans. Even though they had good food in their camps they still liked to come out to eat and I remember a little shop on the bridge, a little restaurant where they knew how to

American troops inside the American Information Bureau. (HRO 65M90/88)

make hamburgers. There used to be a terrific queue to get in and eat an American meal. And the Americans loved our fish and chips. There was a queue from the time they opened to the time they closed.

Joan Halford, née Edmonds, 1926

I think there were more Americans in Winchester than there were British troops. They were very popular because they used to get the girls nylon stockings and chewing gum and cigarettes. When we were in Flowerdown we were invited to some dances that the Americans put on. I went to one of them – I think it was Crawley Court – and they were all

chewing gum. They seemed to have plenty of everything and so of course they were popular. They had more money than the British soldiers which seemed most unfair. British soldiers didn't like it because they were taking all the girls away from them. Actually I didn't like the Americans. I thought they were too forward.

Irene Underwood, née Clewer, 1916

County Information Officer

I was the County Information Officer during the war and as such, was rather adopted by the police because they wanted my loud speaker cars in an emergency and I got as my deputy Colonel Salmon of the Rifle Brigade who lived in St Thomas' Street. The ramifications of the Rifles go all over the county and he came in quite early on. We had to recruit deputies all over the place in collaboration with the police. Before I knew where I was we had deputies all over Hampshire who were ex-Rifle Brigade or Rifle Brigade wives or something. He knew all these people all over the county and roped them in which was very handy really because I didn't know people in places like Havant and all round there. He was a very colourful personality. He used to come in every morning, march up through the works, slap the chaps on the back, 'How are you George? How are you Bill?' and come into my office and salute smartly.'

Monica Woodhouse, née Stroud, 1911

German Bombers overhead

They used to come across Winchester almost every night. You could hear them coming and you used to think oh goodness I hope they go on. And they did used to.

Lilian Woolford, née Hibberd, 1907

German bombers came over us a great deal because their technique was to get over the Itchen, and then follow it down to bomb Southampton. There was no air raid shelter nearby but we had a wonderful vaulted brick cellar which was an ideal place and so we used to let all the inhabitants of St Swithun Street come and shelter in there. It became a very happy centre which they enjoyed awfully. They really were devoted to our cellar.

Then one year come Christmas time they started decorating it and arranging all sorts of beanos, but then the Germans said they weren't going to do any bombing at Christmas so it fell absolutely flat.

Cyril Robinson

Southampton on fire

You could stand here in Winchester and see the fires down in Southampton. You could see the flames from Winchester. The sky was all lit up and you could hear the bombs twelve miles away.

Irene Underwood, née Clewer, 1916

A very busy Life

The blackout was terrible and the food was difficult to manage with, but we were so busy that it all went very quickly in some ways. As a builder my husband had to deal with bomb damage and work on the camps round about. We both did fire watching too. I did it on a Thursday night and had to go out in my tin helmet. It's laughable now but it wasn't at the time. Then when my husband did his turn he had to sleep somewhere down Bar End.

I was involved in a lot of music. There was the church music because our organist was called up and they said, 'Well you'll have to take over.' I said, 'I can't play the organ' but they replied, 'You'll jolly soon have to learn.' Luckily it was only an American organ and being a pianist, I soon got the way of doing the service and all. I was there nearly up until the war ended. Of course there were weddings and occasional

Winchester's fire engine after it was destroyed in a raid on Southampton. The blacksmith Reginald Best lost a son in the incident, as did Mr Chalkley. (HRO 119M84W/1)

funerals there too. Kept me busy. What with taking Miss P. to church in a bath chair too. Pushing her down and pushing her back again in the blackout, with the sirens going and aeroplanes overhead. It was a bit hectic – all up hill. I used to push her from the top of St John's Street right along Beggar's Lane to the little church in Winnall. And then I had to push her back. And then the YMCA used to send down saying, 'We've got a lot of soldiers coming in tonight and we want some amusement for them. Can you do anything about the music?' Oh dear! Out again in the blackout! I did a lot of it. I played for Mr Smithers too. He had a small orchestra in Winchester. We were always playing somewhere or other, either

in the country or here in Winchester.

And I had some evacuees from Portsmouth. The first one was a proper mummy's boy. He was so homesick and his parents were so worried about him that they came and fetched him back after a week. Then I had two more who were much more amenable. More rough and ready and they stayed quite a time. They came up when Portsmouth was bombed badly. There was a really bad night when they bombed Southampton but funnily enough I slept through it all. It was a terrible racket they said. My husband had to go off. He was called out you see. He was gone for about three nights. I didn't recognise him when he came back. He looked so different. He'd been digging

Dorothy Nunn.

people out of the ruins and he looked like an old man after just three nights of it. Terrible. Several people from here were killed who went down with the fire brigades and that. Several people we knew. I couldn't believe my eyes when my husband came in. He was smothered in dirt and his face was all grey and white. Then when my son was eighteen and a half he had to go in the Army. That I do remember. It was an awful thing to see him go off because he was only a schoolboy.

Lilian Woolford, née Hibberd, 1907

A terrible Shock

At one time, Dad used to have to go to Woolston every day to do work on building Spitfires. One night he came home and sat in the armchair white as a sheet. He was so shocked all he kept saying was, 'Poor bloody Southampton!' The night before there had been this big raid and in the morning he had had to walk down the Avenue to get to the ferry because the bus couldn't get through. On the way he saw this little boy sat on a wall. Dad went over to him and said, 'Are you all right nip?' He put his arm out to comfort him and the boy fell into his arms. He was dead. He was sat on this wall. Dead.

Dorothy Nunn, née Bath, 1927

Not going short

My brothers and I, and two or three more men, used to cycle down to Eastleigh and build these air raid shelters all along the road. The women used to come out with jugs of tea and all sorts. We had a fine time. There was one woman down there who had eight youngsters, and so she had a big ration of food. She asked me one day if I would like some bacon and I said I would. So I used to buy half her bacon off her. Then in 1940 we had nothing for Christmas dinner so I went into a butcher's shop in Eastleigh where there was this lovely hand of pork. The butcher said, 'You can't have that. It's booked.' So I said, 'Oh come on. My money's as good as anyone else's' and he let me have it. Before I could bring it home I hid this great hand of pork in one of the air raid shelters and surrounded it with bricks so that nobody would see it. And I used to get a lot of food off of the troops on the camps where I worked. Never went short we didn't. But the bread was terrible.

Ernest Woolford, born 1904

Joan Halford and her husband John. John served thirty-eight and a half years as soldier and civilian with the Greenjackets.

Women's War Effort

Girls going into domestic service – that all stopped because they had to go into war work. There were quite a lot of organizations you could go into once you were seventeen and a half. There was the ATS (the Auxiliary Training Service); the WAAFs (Womens' Army Air Force); the WRENS (Womens' Royal Naval Service), or the NAAFI (Navy, Army and Airforce Institute). Women who hadn't worked since they were married had to go into the shops part-time. Then there was work with ammunition and things. Here in Winchester, it was aircraft. They commandeered the garages for this because they were enormous in those days. Before the war people who owned cars didn't keep them at home but in these garages. I left Woolworth's when I was sixteen to go into aircraft because there was more money.

I went into where we repaired aeroplanes. The training planes were made of wood and I went in as a carpenter's mate. I learnt how to repair the wings and the tail planes. The men were cabinet makers and professional woodworkers who were too old to go in the services. They were very particular and cherished their tools – they had cost them perhaps the equivalent of a year's wages and they kept them immaculate. So of course they didn't like young girls of sixteen using them but when they got confidence in me some of the men did let me. They showed me how to use a chisel, a plane and how to do a join in three ply by 'feathering'. You would have to scrape the edge of the wood

Irene Underwood as Chief Wren in 1942.

Rhoda Biles during her time as a Wren.

so that you saw the three colours and it went on a slope. When you put in on to the plane it was very flat and level. The men were very good to me and I enjoyed working with men more than I did with women. Recently my mother met one of them and he told her I had been one of the best carpenter's mates he'd had working on the aircraft.

Joan Halford, née Edmonds, 1926

Wrens

I applied to become a Wren and wanted to be a wireless operator, so I taught myself morse code by torchlight under the bedclothes during the blackout. After a fourteen-week course at Greenwich I was made up to Chief Wren and posted to Flowerdown. There were two stations there, Y station and W station. Although all our work was sent to Bletchley Park we never knew what W station was doing and I don't suppose they knew what we were doing. We never knew what happened to the information we passed on. We never asked questions. We just did our job and that was it. My mother was living in Winchester and if I had any time off I used to come home and stay with her the night. Winchester was all blacked out, but it was amazing how you could get around. Sometimes for entertainment I used to come into Winchester with other Wrens. There were so many Americans in Winchester that there was always a queue outside the Ritz and the Odeon, so we used to go to the Awdry Tea Rooms. It was above W.H. Smith and Sons. They would have dancing there every night with a three-piece band. There are so many tunes that take me back to those times. Very few civilians you would see in there. They were nearly all soldiers. A few naval men of course. A few Wrens. A lot of ATS girls. All in uniform. If we missed the half-past ten bus back to camp we would walk. We didn't mind – we enjoyed ourselves. After I became an officer I was billeted in North Hill House. I wasn't actually an operator then. My job was to go round and see if the seventy or eighty Wrens and Naval Ratings were doing their job. I wasn't altogether happy as a Wren officer because I would rather do an actual job than just keep my eye on other people. I enjoyed the Service though and if I had my time over again I would have stayed in.

Irene Underwood, née Clewer, 1916

The Russian gun at the entrance to Eastgate Street in 1940, just prior to its removal for scrap in aid of the war effort. (HRO W/C2/5/14)

I volunteered for the Wrens and went to Portsmouth to do my training. The Wren officers were real snobs you know. I wanted to go into office work and be what they called a Writer, but this Wren officer said I hadn't got the right education and told me I could either go in as a messenger or as a cleaner. I thought it was disgusting because I had very good experience, having done a really hard job in the office at Woolworth's and before that, acting as a relief manageress for Pullars of Perth when I was only about seventeen. Well anyway, I went to Flowerdown as a messenger. I hadn't been in very long when I went to the First Officer and asked if I could have a better job to do. I said I was wasting my time. She said, 'How dare you say such a thing? Nobody wastes their time when they are doing their bit for the war effort'. She reported me to the Lieutenant of the Watch and they gave me another job to do which was just as boring as the last one. I told him so when he asked how I was getting on. I spent most of the day knitting. So he put me in the Watch Room with the telegraphists as SDO (Signals Distributing Officer). When the messages came through I used to check them, log them and then take them through to the teleprinters to be sent on to Admiralty. Some of the messages were very important. I had to make sure that they went through quickly because men's lives could be at stake. I absolutely loved that job and my desk was always clear when I went off Watch. You were busy all the time. The Lieutenant came up to me after a while and said, 'Well what's this job like? I suppose you've got too much to do?' I said, 'No Sir. Just the job Sir.' They were the happiest days of my working life.

Rhoda Biles, née Knight, 1921

Social Life of young People

There was no television. There wasn't radios, or only for those who had electricity. For those who didn't have electricity it meant having one of those horrible acid accumulators that you put onto the radio for it to work. Then you had to keep carrying that heavy thing backwards and forwards to the accumulator shop getting it charged up before you could hear your radio. So radio wasn't a big thing during the war for us. Our music really came from going to the dances or the cinema. There was always a queue. By the time you'd finished work and gone and queued up it could be an hour, an hour and a half before you could get in. In fact, you were lucky if you could get in at all sometimes. The last house started about eight o'clock and you didn't always get to see the end of the film either because the soldiers would have to get the last bus to get back to camp. If they'd stayed to see the end they would have had to walk four or five miles back. The Fleet Air Arm boys were the luckiest because they could get the last train from the Great Western Railway at the bottom of the city which left about eleven o'clock and got them back to Worthy Down. They were the last to go. All the other soldiers had to be gone by half past ten. It was nice for us girls, because the

YMCA was right at the top of the town at Newburg House and we would have to walk through the town to get home and get to Highcliffe and Bar End and places like that. The Fleet Air Arm boys used to walk us home, and I used to be dropped off when I got to Colebrook Street, and they'd go over the bridge and get their train. Then a lot of the girls' brothers would meet them at Bar End to take them further on out to their houses at Highcliffe or Fivefields and that. Not that it was necessary to escort us girls home. They were just being friendly and gentlemanly. It was a very nice atmosphere. We were all friends together, because I mean they would come and they would go. Often they were only here for six weeks training and then they'd go to other places. You just made friends with them and danced with them and then they were gone and another lot of troops came in, so you didn't get involved with them.

Joan Halford, née Edmonds, 1926

Strain takes its Toll

My Auntie Alice's husband who was a pilot over at RAF Worthy Down was killed in 1939, just six weeks after the war started. My Auntie Iris' husband Reg was killed when their baby was only fifteen months old. Then in 1941-42 time my grandfather died. He was only fifty-six. He died from lead poisoning from making his own paints. All my grandmother got was ten bob pension. There wasn't even enough money to pay the rent. Nobody owned their houses you see. It was all rent. So each time I went back to grandmother's there was another bit of silver missing that she'd had to sell. She had a very hard life then. There was no help for anybody until 1948 when Social Security came in. Like I say, she had no money, she'd lost her husband, and her two sons-in-law had been killed. Then she had to take in lodgers because she had two spare bedrooms. She had three No. 4 Commandos billeted on her in 1943 but unfortunately they were all killed in the D-Day landings. Well at the end of the war, perhaps because other people were beginning to come back, she just had this terrible nervous breakdown.

Joan Halford, née Edmonds, 1926

CHAPTER 8
After 1945

George Jeger becomes Winchester's first Labour MP

They were treating old ladies for shock in Winchester, but I think people underestimated the real bitterness most of us felt about the 1920s and '30s. The men of the town here had been in the First World War. I worked with them. They used to say, 'Come back to this lot!' They never forgot what happened to them after the war. When the Second World War started, the comment was, 'What the hell's going to happen now? Fight the war and – what?' So it was there all the time. It only wanted picking up and blowing alive. Winchester was different then. They hadn't pulled down all the working class houses in the centre of the town. If you had a political meeting, you had a crowd. We used to have street meetings long before the election. There was a tradition of meetings in the Broadway. We used to go down to Eastgate Street and borrow someone's coal cart and pull it up and stand on that and hold forth. On the night we had our celebration we got slung out of the Guildhall about twelve o' clock but the party went on afterwards in the High Street. They hadn't known anything like it in Winchester. It was the County Surveyor who told me about the old ladies being treated for shock. I said it was a good joke and he said it wasn't a joke. You ask Dr So-and-So, whom I also knew. So I did and he said, 'Oh yes it's perfectly true'. People were coming and saying, 'What's going to happen now doctor? It isn't safe.'

Leslie Greenslade, born c. 1915[25]

Knocking Things down

Winchester has changed out of all recognition. It's been absolutely murdered. Murdered. It's dreadful. I get so angry when I think about it. When I think of all the mistakes they've made. The trouble is that the people who've had the say as to what should be pulled down and what should be built were not Wintonians. As the years went on it was the people who came to Winchester from elsewhere.

Dorothy Yaldren, née Newman, 1903

After my mother died in 1970, the Guildhall wouldn't renew the lease on the umbrella shop premises at twenty-eight the Square. I think they wanted to sell it really. Get rid of it. It was a very old house and I think they'd owned it for about two hundred years. It was an old inn I think before that, because down

Widening the south end of Jewry Street after the demolition of the George Hotel. (HCLS)

in the cellars were some old beer barrels left behind. It was all pulled down, and now part of Boots is on the site. It was quite a character of a house. Lots of old oak beams in it and twelve rooms. We had five rooms, and there was the shop as well which made six. There was another little shop too which my mother used to let to a Mrs Shore who sold antiques and things which went very well with the premises. We had always understood there was a Preservation Order on the building.

Lilian Woolford, née Hibberd, 1907

They pulled down the Brooks just to make car parks, and they pulled down the George Hotel which was where Barclay's is now, to widen the road. All for King Motor Car. I hate 'em. Don't talk to me about cars. Some of the houses in the Brooks were slummy little places but not all of them. There were two or three lovely houses that were pulled down. They were made from some material from the old hospital that used to be on Morn Hill. They were beautiful but the men at the Corporation had it in their heads to

Interior of St Maurice's church before its demolition. (HRO TOP343/2/262)

pull them down because they wanted to make room for motor cars. Old Seymour, what was Health Inspector at the time, he called them slums but they weren't. And where the city's got its office now – a monstrosity if ever there was one – that was all cottages round that area. They were all pulled down to make car parks too. So there you are. Much of Winchester's gone. They pulled St Maurice's down sometime in the fifties. Jenkins and Sons did it. I went there on a Sunday morning and I could have cried when I saw them hitting it down with a big swinging ball. That was a lovely old church. Our son Ernie was christened there. And they pulled down the little church at Winnall where my wife Lily used to play the organ. It was always full. It was right opposite Winnall Moors where they used to have the skating. The College boys used to cut the bank through to flood it so that in the dead of the winter it used to freeze right over. Now it's all occupied by big firms.

Ernest Woolford, born 1904

No I don't feel sad about them knocking down the houses in the Brooks. I think its time had come. Some of the places were absolute hovels they really were, and I think the older people had had enough of it. They were building the council houses and the younger people – the ones my age – couldn't wait to get somewhere decent. But when they moved the people out to the council houses the character went out of the centre of the town.

Lousia Lewis, née Salter, 1918

Turning away from the Church

They thought that with the estate at Winnall they would want a bigger church but they didn't. People didn't come to church any more. In my time you might say the church did everything. If you wanted a club or anything it was always the church you turned to. There was the Men's Society and the Mothers' Union and things like that, and nearly always you'd start off with a service in the church. And the vicar or the vicar's wife would be chairman or president of the club. Oh yes the church kind of ran everything in those days. Even to string orchestras. I used to like a string orchestra in the church. Most of my childhood I was in the choir at St John's but when my voice broke they wanted an organist at Winnall so I went there. It was a harmonium really and I went backwards and forwards for eighteen years. I reckon I wore out Wales Street! I used to do that evenings, twice every Sunday and three times at festivals. But I liked doing it. I always looked forward to that. It was a happy, cosy little church. Just pews either side and a small altar at the far end. It had just one bell over the font and a very, very small vestry. There was about room for the parson and one other person. Whenever there was a wedding they had to go in one at a time to sign the register. I was married there, and my only child was christened there. The wife's mother was churchwarden and used to ring the bell. But it's gone now. They pulled it down. They don't think anything of religion now.

Jesse Smith, born 1903

St Martin's church at Winnall before its demolition. (HRO 147M87/1/3513)

The Winchester Herald

No. 2   MARCH, 1948.   Price 2d.

THE NATIONAL UNION OF AGRICULTURAL WORKERS
A Remarkable Trade Union Achievement

FOR the third year in succession Hampshire farm workers invaded the City of Winchester on February 28th and marched into possession of the Guildhall for their **annual celebrations.** Headed by a brass band, and with colours flying, the men and women most truly representative of Hampshire's principal industry demonstrated their ability to organise and act for the common good.

Assembled to hear addresses from their General Secretary, Mr. A. C. Dann, Mr. George Jeger, M.P., and Organiser " Bob " Allcorn, to play off the County Darts Tournament and have a good time, the Union's members, as Britain's first barrier against starvation, were given a hearty welcome to the City. We well remember, when some three years ago this thousand-strong march began, the shock of surprise which ran round the City as it realised for the first time that the countryside was rising.

War may have brought its tragedies, but it also brought a new importance and force of life to the countryside. An agriculture reflected in thistle-covered fields, mouldering cottages and abandened farm buildings, the Hampshire of our heritage, is rebuilt again into a living organism. For farm workers there has been a great mental stride forward from the degradation of decay and the closed hand of an outworn feudalism.

Behind the physical force of this demonstration lies a firstclass job of Trade Union organisation. Central character of this has been Organiser " Bob "

General Secretary A. C. Dann, Organiser Bob Allcorn and George Jeger, M.P., discussing the "Winchester Herald".

Allcorn, who first came to Hampshire in 1941. Then, a year after Dunkirk, when farmers were clearing uplands and considering the ploughing of pastures, only a handful of Union members, a meagre 400 diehards, could be found. Victimisation, lack of progressive agricultural policy, isolation, fear and mistrust had been the dark history of the years between the wars. Cheap labour, tied cottages and redundancy are not good soil for the growth of free men.

Tackling the job with characteristic cheerfulness, Bob Allcorn set out to build an organisation. We well remember Bob and his old Morris Eight, late nights and breakdowns, never-ceasing journeys, constantly planning more Branch-opening meetings, and Mrs. Allcorn, too, taking the rough with the smooth.

Gathering a small crowd of active workers, R. Dean of Froyle, now Berkshire Organiser, F. Cresswell, also of Froyle, whose death in January was mourned by all Union members, friends Shuttler and Hooper of Fordingbridge, Lloyd Lewis, of Basingstoke in those days, Janet Davis of Thruxton, W. Whitcher of Hawkley, A. Wither of Hambledon, G. G. Griffin of Bramdean, T. Hillier of Swanwick, A. G. Fletcher of Micheldever, and many others, the Union was steadily built up into a force. From 12 Branches in 1941 to just under 100 in 1948, from 400 members to over 6,000 members, Branches which have penetrated into every corner of the county.

Government interest in agriculture from the first day of war was a necessity. Interest in farming must include interest in the

workers if a happy state of affairs is to be reached. Workers who unite and express their demands in no uncertain voice must be fully considered and the seed of these early days has yielded a good harvest.

Wages have risen from 32s. 6d. to 90s.

Hours have been reduced from an average 50 to a settled 48.

Where no holidays existed before the war now six days' annual holiday and six public holidays apply.

Increased production per man is estimated at over 15%.

From almost no representation on public bodies the Union is now perhaps the most widely represented body of its kind in the county, with seats on R.D.C. Housing Committees, Local Employment Committees, Agricultural Education, Rural District Councils and Parish Councils, the County Council Smallholding Committee, the Growmore Clubs, the Young Farmers' Club. Under the Agricultural Executive Committee it has two seats on the Executive Committee itself and one in each of the seven District Committees. It has three seats on the County Wages Committee, is represented on the Regional Council for County Roadmen and the Forestry Joint Industrial Council.

Its democratic system of self-government develops from the Branch to the four District Committees on to the County Committee, with the Union's National Conference as the supreme body. In 1941 the County Committee was almost without funds. To-day it disburses some £500 a year and is entirely self-financing.

The Legal Department of the Union has played a most important part in the county. In five years over £10,000 has been secured as compensation. In the first three months of 1948 alone some £2,000 has been won for its members. Through its association with the Winchester Divisional Labour Party the Union secured, in the name of that Party, the inclusion of a resolution on the Agenda of the 1947 Labour Party Conference condemning the continuation of the tied cottage system, and pledging the Government to secure the removal of this mark of serfdom. The resolution was adopted by Conference. Setting out to win over both employing and Government representatives it has, through the wages machine, established the principle of national wage rates.

From a small, though loyal, group has grown a dynamic force capable of bold and successful representation—a force which is still growing. And yet, like slugs beneath the unturned stone, there may yet be found those miserable specimens who can still bleat, " Why should I join the Union ? What has it done for me ? "

A Goliath has grown from this David. Good luck, farm workers.

Issue No. 2 of 'The New Local Labour and Trade Union Monthly', published in March 1948. In the centre is George Jeger, Winchester's first and only Labour MP.

Building of Stanmore, Weeke and Winnall

Dad worked on the Winnall houses. We used to go out for these compulsory Sunday walks. He used to trudge us all through Chilcomb and down through the water meadows and all sorts of places, but one day he took us to Morn Hill. I can remember standing at the top of Winnall Manor Road and looking down it and there were probably eight houses. Lots of building work going on. Lots of places that were marked out. He showed us where he was working. It was terribly posh at the time to get a house at Winnall. They were lovely houses compared to ours. We thought everyone who got a house at Winnall was really lucky.

Annette Hawkins, née Gough, 1949

German prisoners of war made the roads and foundations for the new houses they built at Stanmore. Then when Weeke started being built and people in the town heard they were going to plough all the trees up and everything to turn it into houses, they went up there with their prams and pushchairs to collect all the apples and all the fruit. It was sad really, but they've made quite a nice estate of Weeke. I've lived at Stanmore and I've lived at Winnall in the council-owned houses and I've been very happy with them.

Joan Halford, née Edmonds, 1926

Coming Home to the Weirs

My mother and her sister Dolly were born in one of the little houses that stood by the Weirs. When Aunt Dolly was six years old she fell in the river there. She couldn't swim and so she was frightened and splashing about. Somebody called to her and she looked up and there was a man standing in the 'horseshoe' – the horseshoe shaped piece of brickwork in front of the mill. He was fishing about with a pole and called to her to grab it. As she reached towards it he kept moving the pole a little bit further away. She was making strokes and in a short while she suddenly realised she was actually swimming. She loved it and after that you just couldn't keep her out of the water! Eventually she left Winchester and settled in Bradford, but her roots went very deep here. Right into her old age, every time she came to stay she insisted on going to the Weirs, peeling off her stockings and dabbling her feet. The last year she came she

Annette Hawkins, the youngest of Victor Gough's four daughters. (PG)

was in a lot of pain but again she felt compelled to do the same thing. That year the river was down and she couldn't actually reach the water, so we took her to Water Lane and sort of hung her over the wall so she could get her feet wet. She was so happy there, swinging her legs. That year too, at the 'horseshoe' on the Weirs, she leant over the edge and said to my husband and me, 'When I die this is where I want to go. Not over that side but over this side where the mill race is. I want to go in here because this is where I fell in all those years ago and was saved from. If the river wanted me it can have me.' So a couple of years later when she died her family brought her down from Bradford. About thirty of us trekked down to the Weirs, carrying her ashes. It was really quite touching because we all stood there in the 'horseshoe' and dropped flowers over the side for her and said our goodbyes, and told her where she was. It was really quite sweet. She was seventy-five and every time she came back to Winchester she had to dabble her feet.

Annette Hawkins, née Gough, 1949

Wharf Mill on the Weirs in the late 1960s. Gertrude Asher's father had helped to build it in the 1880s, but in 1967 it ceased work, and in 1972 was converted into luxury flats. The brickwork which protrudes into the water is 'the horseshoe' and it was from the water to the left as you look at the picture that Annette Hawkin's Aunt Dolly was saved. (HCLS)

Notes

1. The Itchen Navigation or 'canal' was an 'improved river' which carried its last barge in 1869. Its 'most important traffic was coal, trans-shipped from the collier brigs from the north-east coast at Northam, and taken up to Winchester at Blackbridge Wharf... the value of the Navigation lay only partly in its transport function; it was also important for winter irrigation and summer drainage of the adjoining water meadows. This involved the manipulation of the hatches or sluices in the banks of the canal, a frequent source of controversy between the proprietors and the riparian landowners and tenants.' See 'The Itchen Navigation' by Edwin Course in Volume 24 of the *Proceedings of the Hampshire Field Club and Archaeological Society*.

2. The first train arrived at the lower station in 1885 and the last passenger train left in 1960. The station was originally referred to as 'Cheesehill' but was renamed 'Chesil' in September 1949. 'Cheesehill Street' had already been changed to the more authentic 'Chesil Street' in about 1914. 'Chesil' derives from the Anglo-Saxon *ceosel*, meaning 'gravel', and refers to a bank of pebbles by the River Itchen.

3. The Hockley Viaduct was completed in 1891 to link the Didcot Newbury and Southampton line with the London and South Western at Shawford Junction.

4. This densely populated area was considered by its inhabitants and others to be the heart of the city. Lying north of the lower part of the High Street and comprising Upper Brook Street, Middle Brook Street and Lower Brook Street, it was almost entirely demolished in the 1950s. Colebrook Street, on the opposite side of the High Street, was also considered to be part of the Brooks. Many of its houses were likewise destroyed in post-war 'slum' clearance.

5. The Suffolk Arms used to be in the High Street where Marks and Spencer is now situated.

6. Thomas Stopher 1835-1926. Architect and Alderman who took an active part in civic life for over fifty-three years. He was Mayor of Winchester in 1877, 1884 and 1894. Keenly interested in the arts and education, he was particularly associated with the establishment of a public library and the School of Art.

7. A photograph of Old Dad is reproduced in *In and Around Winchester in Old Photographs* by Edward Roberts, 1977.

8. The Revd H.C. Dickens had been the incumbent of St John's since 1871.

9. William Walker worked beneath the cathedral from April 1906 until September 1911. At the end of 1912 he was summoned to Buckingham Palace to receive the Royal Victorian Order. The statue by Sir Charles Wheeler unveiled in 1964 and placed in Winchester cathedral was mistakenly of Frances Fox, an engineer whose services were also engaged in saving the cathedral and who received a Knighthood for them. See *The Winchester Diver – the Saving of a Great Cathedral* by Ian T. Henderson and John Crook, 1984. In June 2001 the statue of Fox was replaced by one of Walker executed by Glyn

Williams. It can be seen just outside the Lady Chapel on the south side.

10. The visit is reported by the *Hampshire Chronicle* to have lasted a mere six minutes and to have taken place on 20 July 1897. The Queen was travelling from Windsor to Osborne, and the Royal Train halted at the down platform of the LSWR station. Her Majesty remained in her specially designed carriage with her chair turned so that she could look out through open double doors towards Mayor Harry Webb as he delivered a Loyal Address from a dais on the platform. It has been suggested that the brevity of the visit was due to some ill feeling between the Queen and the Bishop of Winchester

11. See *Hampshire Papers* No. 17 published by Hampshire County Council, 1999. 'The King Alfred Millenary in Winchester, 1901' by Barbara Yorke.

12. The Winchester National Pageant was held in the final six days of June 1908 in order to raise funds for the repair work being carried out on the cathedral. Following its completion in 1912, a whole week was devoted to services of thanksgiving. The main one was held on St Swithun's Day, July 15, when King George V and Queen Mary were in attendance.

13. The Gun Riots. The gun concerned was captured from the Russians at Sevastapol during the Crimean War of 1854-56. It was presented to the city by Lord Panmure as part of the celebrations for what was believed to be the seven-hundredth anniversary of the mayorality in 1884. In 1885 the corporation moved it to the top of St Giles Hill. Infuriated townspeople returned it to the entrance to Eastgate Street and were helped to do so by navvies constructing the Didcot Newbury and Southampton Railway. Although newspaper and other accounts of the events of late May 1908 tell us what happened, they do not explain quite why tempers ran so high. It would seem that the gun was felt to symbolize the freedoms of the townspeople and to belong to them rather than to 'government' as represented by the mayor and corporation. This may have been at least partly due to the role played by the Rifle Brigade at Sevastapol and the losses sustained by it during the Crimean War. Faced by the consequences of his high-handedness the then mayor, Alderman Forder, backed down and the gun and its railings were replaced. See *Hampshire Chronicle* 30 May 1908. However in August 1940 when Winchester City Council adopted a proposal from Alderman Sankey and the General Purposes Committee that the gun and its railings should be removed for scrap in aid of the war effort, the decision excited little or no attention.

14. The Weirs is a footpath on the west side of the Itchen, running south from City Bridge towards Wharf Hill

15. *Domum* is Latin for 'homewards'. *Dulce Domum* is the title of the College song sung at the end of the school year. See *Winchester Notions – The English Dialect of Winchester College* by Charles Stevens, 1998.

16. The Revd John Henry Bromby Mace had become Rector of Holy Trinity in 1925.

17. The Barracks fire broke out on the morning of 19 December 1894.

18. Malise Archibald Cunningame Graham who died in 1885 aged twenty-five.

19. George V made his first visit to Winchester when, as Prince of Wales, he attended the unveiling of the window in the cathedral to the memory of the Riflemen who fell in the South African War.

20. Malaria

21. This picture appeared (No. 75) in Edward Roberts *In and Around Winchester in Old Photographs*, 1977. At that time the author believed it to show soldiers called in by police to quell a riot. He was later reliably informed that the soldiers had been harassing a butcher and that police were called in to quell the soldiers.

22. Lord Edward Derby 1865-1948. In an attempt to avoid the introduction of conscription, the Derby Scheme asked all eligible males for voluntary 'assent' to service if called upon, promising that married men would be called last. The scheme was abandoned in December 1915 having provided fewer than 350,000 potential troops.

23. The Riflemens' Cottages are in Greenjacket Close off Stanmore Lane.

24. This actually took place in Romford, Essex. Dorothy Yaldren was living there in 1939 when her husband was stationed at a nearby RAF camp. I thought the event could just as easily have happened in Winchester and that the story was too good to omit.

25. Leslie Greenslade was a full-time trade union official who, together with Ted Hibberd, acted as Jeger's Agent during the 1945 campaign. See *Southern History* Volume 8/1986 – 'The Labour Victory in Winchester in 1945' by Sarah Bussy.

Acknowledgements

HC   *Hampshire Chronicle*
HCLS   Hampshire County Library Service
HRO   Hampshire Record Office
IWM   Imperial War Museum
WCL   Winchester Cathedral Library
WMS   Winchester Museum Service
DN   Dorothy Nunn
EAS   E.A. Sollars
LL   Louisa Lewis
PG   Philip Gough

I should like most particularly to express my gratitude to David Lee of the Wessex Film and Sound Archive for all the help he has given me with the preparation of this book. Sincere thanks are similarly due to Gill Rushton at the Hampshire Record Office, and to Philippa Stevens at the Local Studies Department of the County Library.

Although every attempt has been made to trace the copyright holders of photographs reproduced here I must apologise for those instances where this has not proved possible. However I gratefully acknowledge permission to use material belonging to the Hampshire Record Office, the Hampshire County Library Service/ D.G. Dine, the *Hampshire Chronicle*, the Imperial War Museum, Winchester Cathedral Library, Winchester City Council and Winchester Museum Service. I am also indebted to Warren and Sons Ltd for allowing me to reproduce material from their Winchester Directories of 1906, 1915 and 1938, and to Trevor Evans for photographic work. Special thanks are also due to Maurice McGrave for help with research. I am also grateful to Alan Cleaver – Editor of the *Hampshire Chronicle*, Michael Jackson – Director of St John's Charity, Dr R. Custance – Archivist at Winchester College, Bill Peterson, Kevin Robertson, Barry Richardson, Edward Roberts and Ann Wadman.

Above all though I must thank some of the many people who have welcomed me into their homes, have allowed me to record their memories, have lent me their family photographs and have not only shown me the utmost kindness but been enormously helpful in every way – Rhoda Biles, Ben Kerley, Joan and John Halford, Annette Hawkins, Louisa Lewis, Dorothy and Ernest Nunn and Irene and Norman Underwood.